Helen Mirren

PRIME SUSPECT

A Celebration

Helen Mirren

PRIME SUSPECT

A Celebration

———

EDITED BY AMY RENNERT

Design by Louise Kollenbaum

KQED
BOOKS

SAN FRANCISCO

Vice President for Publishing & New Ventures: Mark K. Powelson

Publisher: Pamela Byers
Editor: Amy Rennert
Book and Cover Design: Louise Kollenbaum
Managing Editor: Sharon Epel
Associate Editor: Pamela Feinsilber

Production Director: Bradford Stauffer
Production: John Walker
Research Assistant: Allyson Quibell
Printing Services: *Penn&Ink Hong Kong*

KQED President & CEO: Mary G. F. Bitterman

Prime Suspect photographs supplied courtesy of Granada Television Limited. The *Prime Suspect* title is owned by Granada Television and is used with its express permission. Permissions and other text and photo credits will be found on page 139.

Educational and nonprofit groups wishing to order this book at attractive quantity discounts may contact KQED Books & Tapes, 2601 Mariposa St., San Francisco, CA 94110.

Library of Congress Cataloging-in-Publication Data
Helen Mirren: Prime Suspect : a celebration / edited by Amy Rennert.
p.   cm.
ISBN 0-912333-69-3
1. Mirren, Helen. 2. Prime Suspect (Television program)
I. Rennert, Amy.
PN2598.M565H46 1995   95-24944
791.45'72--dc20   CIP

ISBN 0-912333-69-3

Printed in Hong Kong
10 9 8 7 6 5 4 3 2 1

On the cover: Helen Mirren as Detective Chief Inspector Jane Tennison, courtesy Granada Television Limited

Distributed to the trade by Publishers Group West

For Ellen Rennert and Charlotte Kollenbaum

Two Leading Ladies

table of contents

introduction

By Amy Rennert

RECENT ACADEMY AWARD nominee and winner of the Cannes Best Actress award for *The Madness of King George*. Tony nominee for her Broadway debut in *A Month in the Country*. Eagerly awaited by legions of fans longing to see her Jane Tennison in action again. This must be the prime of Ms. Helen Mirren. With three new installments of *Prime Suspect* slated for television through 1996, what better time to celebrate her many accomplishments?

Long acclaimed in England for her classic and contemporary roles on stage and renowned for some adventurous film roles, Mirren gained almost overnight fame in the US with the Public Broadcasting Service's airing of *Prime Suspect* in 1992. This exceptional miniseries about a female cop pursuing a serial killer as she fights sexism in the London police department earned several television awards in Great Britain and won high marks from critics on both sides of the Atlantic. It also achieved the best ratings of the season for *Mystery!*, the program that televised the series in this country. Twelve million people tuned in.

No one would accuse Detective Chief Inspector Jane Tennison of being perfect. But she is the most realistic, multidimensional woman on the screen—film or television. She's strong one moment and vulnerable the next. She's tender with one colleague; she rides roughshod over another. She stands up to authority, but she'll compromise to advance her career. Her professional success is hard-won; her private life is a mess. She's no Miss Marple.

It's the complexity of Mirren's characterization, and the extent to which she gives herself over to the role, that makes her Jane Tennison so compelling. Mirren never lets her character display the predictable response. In her every gesture, however small, she portrays Tennison's emotions in a way that reveals something about her and, often simultaneously, brings into focus something new about the situation. Mirren's no-nonsense police detective also exudes plenty of sexual charisma. Rarely have we seen such a sustained performance or had such an opportunity to watch a character change over time.

Over the years, I have had the opportunity to interview dozens of remarkable artists. Mirren is the only one who seems to intrigue men and women in equal numbers. Her admirers can't seem to get enough of her.

If you're one of them, this book is for you. In the pages that follow, you'll be drawn to the many faces of this actress—Mirren adores the camera and vice versa—and you'll discover insightful analyses of her television, film, and theatrical work by leading critics. I was able to track down one of her closest friends, a journalist who contributes a lively and revealing personal essay, along with photos from her scrapbook. And, in an extensive interview, Mirren herself talks about her work and her life.

I am grateful to Ms. Mirren for the time she spent with me in New York, Los Angeles, and London, and for her participation in this project. I can hardly wait to see where she turns up next.

Amy Rennert with Helen Mirren

an appreciation
By James Wolcott

HE MOVIE SCREEN MAY BE larger than the television screen, but it has become a tiny portal—a prison window—for any actress valuing her talent and sanity. As movies imitate the apocalyptic effects of video games and doomsday machines, filmmakers have abandoned the flirty looks, snappy dialogue, and relaxed camaraderie the sexes used to share in romantic comedies and serious dramas. Now it's every cyborg for itself out there in the killing zone. Movies are seldom actress-driven these days, as they were from the thirties to the fifties, when the cement fright mask of Joan Crawford could plow through a noble tearjerker, or Audrey Hepburn's scarf could sign the air in *Funny Face* with jaunty esprit. Even in the seventies, Jane Fonda could supply the energy

source for *Klute*. The romantic heroines today have cream puffs for cheekbones (Goldie Hawn and Meg Ryan—Twinkies separated from the same plastic wrapper), while the serious actresses nurse an inner insecurity that reveals itself in an excessive play of voice inflection and fidgety mannerisms. (Blushing before Clint Eastwood in *The Bridges of Madison County*, Meryl Streep does so much business with her hands, she seems to be building a bird's nest in her hair.) A woman must be willing to pick up a gun to find work as a Hollywood actress, unless she's willing to employ her body as a weapon, as Sharon Stone did with the stretchy limbs and sassy crotch of a Bob Fosse dancer in *Basic Instinct*, or employ her mouth like a smoke-ring machine, à la Linda Fiorentino in *The Last Seduction*. What's missing on the movie screen for actresses is the everyday range of reality and experience—social terrain they could inhabit and navigate like characters in a novel.

Out from under the blockbuster imperatives of Hollywood, the oppressive bulk of all that money and meddling, some actresses have found refuge fending for themselves in the more intimate confines of TV. With few exceptions, the great acting being done by women today is on television, not just in such obvious prestige performances as Vanessa Redgrave's in *Playing for Time*, but in the mundane byways of the made-for-cable movie, where Mare Winningham worries the insides of her everyday-heroine roles, wearing the face of a woman in a Dorothea Lange photograph, and the amusing, sporty Virginia Madsen shifts her hips through a series of suspense twists. (Before she became a superbimbo, Kim Basinger did her most luminous, least cluttered acting in forgettable TV flicks.)

On television, where the close-up dominates, an actress can still hold the camera through force of personality. She needn't even strike a goddess pose, like Garbo or Dietrich achieving a blank bliss state in some old war-horse from the archives. A glamour puss like Joanna Lumley in the British sitcom *Absolutely Fabulous* need only drag her lips over her horsey teeth to create a cracked-mirror image of beauty gone haywire. TV is a behavioral medium that requires the actor to react and relate to buzzing stimuli from all sides. (That's why Faye Dunaway flopped on TV—she thought she could still play statue.)

Probably no actress has made a bolder push on television and demonstrated keener instincts for pulling off an inside job than Helen Mirren in the British police series *Prime Suspect*, created by Lynda La Plante. As Detective Chief Inspector Jane Tennison, Mirren always has her feelers out, keeping her character in the present tense. Mirren's face seems composed of news-photo pixels—a mesh of dots. It is an information screen on which we read her reactions to flippant comments from her colleagues or bad news from the field. The murders on *Prime Suspect* are tabloid horrors (serial killers torture their female victims in makeshift dungeons like de Sade, or bury bodies in backyard gardens), but Tennison's methodical mind marshals and abstracts the details of the case until they click like the beads of an abacus. Each case is also a test of character, a new gauntlet to walk. Where Cagney and Lacey practically fall over each other to show they're caring lugs (they chew their dialogue as if eating their way to the bottom of a lunch bag), Tennison maintains a clipped conduct, a strict posture that both emphasizes professional dispatch and slightly parodies it. She has irony down to a fine inflection.

Such constraint allows Mirren to consolidate her force onscreen in ways that flashier roles in the past let squander. Born in 1946, Mirren learned her craft as a stage actress in Great Britain, performing the ripe plums of classical repertory. She has

"I have always considered myself serious about what I do, but I hate the phrase 'serious actress.' It's important not to take yourself too seriously, to be able to laugh at yourself."

—HELEN MIRREN
1985

been lauded as a "mature" actress for so long that it's a shock to view her early movies (*Savage Messiah*, *O Lucky Man!*) and see how lush yet scissory she looked in her early days. Her roles did not expand on film until she essayed characters whose flesh was beginning to sour. When her characters misbehaved, it wasn't because they were overcome by delirious abandon; they had made a conscious decision to be bad (you could tell from their determined eyes). Mirren became known for playing soul-sick Eurotrash, leftover dollops from the era of *la dolce vita*. She was a gangster's moll in *The Long Good Friday*, a decadent bird of prey in *The Cook, the Thief, His Wife and Her Lover*, a grape-popping pagan in the porn epic *Caligula*; she even played Christopher Walken's wife in *The Comfort of Strangers*—it doesn't get any weirder than that (Walken could have given Caligula lessons). Her movie career hasn't been all art-house hanky-panky. She brought a nicotine drive and a smoldering regret to the Russian ballerina role in *White Nights* (she resembled Natalya Makarova, minus the gypsy smile), suffered Harrison Ford's messiah complex as the harried wife in *The Mosquito Coast*, was resplendent as Morgana in *Excalibur*.

In each outing, Mirren led with her chin. Nothing disturbed her poise onscreen; she made challenging eye-contact with her costars, maintaining a no-trespass zone in the severity of her gaze. Her tremendous focus made everyone else seem half there. But she was in danger of dehydrating onscreen by having to deny so much of her acting palette—by being a functional pro in other people's sagas. Her face often looked parched.

Prime Suspect enabled Mirren to make the most of her stiletto manner and convert it into a feminist statement about the crappy sacrifices a woman makes for her career. What made the first *Prime Suspect* especially timely in this country was that it followed

so closely on the Clarence Thomas-Anita Hill hearings. The raw nerves Hill touched in her harassment testimony during Thomas' Supreme Court confirmation hearings were laid out like a network of tripwires on *Prime Suspect*. When a male inspector dies of a heart attack during the investigation of a prostitute's rape-murder (Forensics: "I reckon she's got semen in virtually every orifice"), Mirren's Tennison lobbies for the case. The only woman of senior status in the department, she's tired of being a desk jockey; she wants a juicy corpse to juggle. (An attitude echoed in a later *Prime Suspect*, where another dead body liberates her from the drudgery of shuffling paper.) She's approved for the assignment only after a superior pays her the ultimate accolade. With a purr, he says she has "balls."

Once she assumes command of the murder squad, however, she meets with nothing but obstruction—a lumpy mass of smug male inertia. She's like a substitute teacher in a classroom full of instigators. Each day she meets a chorus of smirks. With mock deference, the men call her "ma'am," not that they mind their manners; when she slips in the mud, no one offers assistance. Without preaching, *Prime Suspect* does a peerless job of showing how men belittle women in a small multitude of ways, how men use sidelong looks and inside humor to screen them out of the action. A woman I know who has directed documentaries for the BBC says that the cops in *Prime Suspect* remind her of all the all-male film crews she used to have to cajole: slow-moving, always muttering under their breaths, a collective mule to motivate. (And it was Norman Mailer who noted the resemblance between film crews and off-duty cops—"the same heavy meat on the shoulders, same bellies oiled on beer.") The older men in Tennison's department all look like oil paintings, with their embalmed cheeks and veiny noses.

What Mirren did, I suspect, was use the apprehension and opportunity of being one of the few women on the set to express Tennison's own embattled condition in this testosterone ward. Like Tennison, Mirren had to hit the workplace cold.

"I literally finished in Italy at four o'clock, where I was filming *Where Angels Fear to Tread*, flew to England, had my hair chopped off, and started *Prime Suspect* the next morning," she told one interviewer. Her portrayal of Tennison shows a similar clipped, adaptive spirit. She must prove herself battle-ready, worth the mettle of any man. In scenes in which she has to report to her superiors or conduct a formal interrogation of a subject, Tennison prepares before the mirror like a player putting on his game-face. She applies her lipstick like war-paint and then—her defining gesture—straightens herself, tugging and smoothing the front of her jacket to complete her presentation. She seems to snap herself into place. Forced to accept an earful from an irate male superior, Tennison stands at attention and clicks her head to the side, listening as if she has a meter running inside her head. She honors the outward forms like a soldier saluting a little too crisply, that extra snap serving as a declaration of independence. In an enclosed hierarchy like the police establishment, even body language must be in code.

Only when she addresses the "lads" can she loosen her armor. One of *Prime Suspect*'s sequences has Tennison ticking off the grisly points of the investigation as she snacks from a bag of crisps. As she hits her mental stride, the lads lose some of the lead in their drawers and hop to it. Asked in an interview if she enjoyed bossing a roomful of men, Mirren replied, "I did. I absolutely loved it." It shows. Tennison beams when her boys bring her clues. She acquires the charisma of a lioness.

After the critical and popular success of the first *Prime*

Suspect, a success due not only to Mirren's breakthrough performance but to brilliant support work by John Bowe as the mousy suspect George Marlow and Zoe Wanamaker as his harridan wife, a sequel was inevitable. "*Prime Suspect 2* was not as good," David Thomson commented in his *Biographical Dictionary of Film*, "but who could deny Helen Mirren her franchise?" Who, indeed? Only all of Hollywood. Universal Studios optioned the rights for a movie version that would be revamped for a "bankable" American actress. *Prime Suspect* fans feared that La Plante's hardy original would be defanged, and declawed, and turned into a stuffed mascot, a fate that befell the audacious English miniseries *The Life and Loves of a She-Devil*, dumbed down into a pointless travesty starring Meryl Streep and Roseanne. Not surprisingly, Mirren feels territorial about the role of Tennison. She has said, "Tell Universal I'll be very pissed off if Jane Fonda or anyone else plays the part. It's mine."

As the big-screen *Prime Suspect* project went nowhere, American television seized the initiative with the series *Under Suspicion* (CBS), starring Karen Sillas. Although the premise mimicked *Prime Suspect*'s, the show took place on a planet of denser gravity. *Under Suspicion* abjured the naturalistic cubbyhole bustle of *Prime Suspect* for a film noir atmosphere of steep-angled shadows and cones of dusty sunlight. Amid the shadows were dark shapes purported to be the cast, who remained stationary so that they wouldn't disturb the show's Kafkaesque mood and be mistaken for actual people. No mouths could be spotted moving as one silhouette interrogated another. As the top female detective, Sillas, who won critical acclaim in the lonelyhearts film *What Happened Was...*, carried such a thick load of earnest intention that she seemed glacial and even more static than the shadows. Where Mirren had a coat of ice, Sillas was a block of ice.

"I've always had a sneaking suspicion that I'm going to be much better when I get older. I think that suits me better."
—HELEN MIRREN
1971

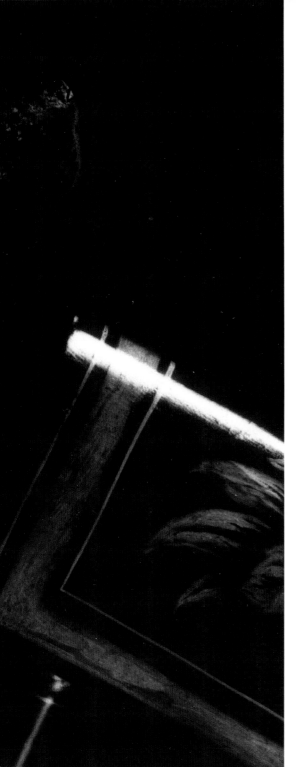

"I can't under-
stand why forty
was supposed to be
so traumatic.
One's confidence
in one's achieve-
ments and physical
appearance comes
and goes from week
to week all
through one's
life."

—HELEN MIRREN
1991

With the *Prime Suspect* movie in development limbo and *Under Suspicion* limping in the ratings, Mirren has a mortal lock on Jane Tennison as role model and popcult icon. But the very triumph of *Prime Suspect* as Mirren's charisma showcase creates its own predicament: How does Tennison maintain her underdog status when the actress who plays her is so obviously the show's driving force? It doesn't take much quality decline for a star vehicle to become a transparent contraption. Eddie Murphy could play the outsider semi-believably in the first *Beverly Hills Cop*, but the premise became harder to sustain once he became a superstar; his cocky sense of prerogative fenced him off from the other actors every time he flashed his bankroll smile. By *Lethal Weapon III*, Mel Gibson was presiding like the owner of his own amusement park.

True, Mirren radiates no aura of entitlement. Working off the camera like a fighter who digs from the inside, she rubs all vanity off the role of Tennison to show the grainy surface underneath, the pitted face of fatigue. But there's an unevenness in the way Tennison is treated in the sequels to *Prime Suspect*, an uncertainty as to how much clout she should carry, how much resistance she should confront. The filmmakers seem to make an effort to muffle her magnetism, subordinating her to the overall integrity of the piece. Of course, the series would have become monotonous had it continued to have Tennison prove herself on each outing, but with each sequel comes a thicker coating of urban sociology, as if Tennison were a dipstick to measure the depths of despair. (*Prime Suspect 3* narrowly avoided being a voyeuristic exposé of the clammy callboy trade through the toxic presence of David Thewlis, the star of Mike Leigh's *Naked*, whose predatory walk had more menace than most actors' psycho extremes.)

With three new two-hour *Prime Suspect* television movies,

the series threatens to settle down to being a familiar import, like the adventures of Maigret, Poirot, or Inspector Morse but with more punch and squalor. (Tennison's losing battle to give up smoking almost becomes a cozy quirk.) Each is a complete story, done by a different director. The first mystery, "The Lost Child," a mossy and suitably mournful study in pedophilia, lurches into conventional cop melodrama when a motorcycle conveniently slams into an ambulance carrying the suspect, he escapes, and there's a protracted siege, complete with sniper units; "Inner Circles," which begins with a kinky case, becomes a too-obvious bifocal look at the English class system, the snobbish country-club set versus the yobs. It is the last drama— "The Scent of Darkness"—that rescues the franchise and brings us full circle.

The case involves the abduction-torture-murder of women by a killer who has modeled his M.O. on that of George Marlow, the killer in the first *Prime Suspect*. Since Marlow is still behind bars, this killer is either a copycat or the true original. If he is the original murderer, then Marlow is innocent—and Tennison's career was built upon a miscarriage of justice. Tennison has to prove herself all over again, justify her hounding of Marlow into prison. The more zealously she argues that she was right the first time, the more defensive and tendentious she seems. She refuses to admit even the possibility that she scalped the wrong man. (The other officers exchange Knowing Glances every time she becomes vehement.) By reopening Tennison's first case and casting doubt on her infallibility, *Prime Suspect* recaptures the brainy ambiguity that made it a perfect fit for Mirren. The story seems calibrated to the flicker of her thoughts, in sync with her own excitement.

What may disturb *Prime Suspect* devotees is the development

"My hero is Gerard Depardieu. I like the way he takes whatever comes along—lawyer, gangster, anything. If the part calls for him to be naked, off comes his shirt. He doesn't worry about looking gorgeous. That's what I admire. A lack of vanity."

—HELEN MIRREN
1994

in Tennison's personal life as she takes on a serious lover, a psychologist named Patrick Schofield (Stuart Wilson), who first surfaces in the pedophile episode. (You can tell she's smitten because her hair looks so fleecy.) Some viewers have such an investment in Jane Tennison as a tough cookie making her way solo in the world that they may not accept her slouching towards domesticity, snuggling with a professional who patronizes her with a martyred sigh of extorted patience, as if he were trying to reason with an irrational woman. Tennison is not long subdued. The film ends with a diva flourish as one of the male louses in the department insults her in public with a sexist remark—which she answers by flinging a drink at the whole lot of them. It isn't the flash of temper that makes the scene so bravura, it's the pure dare on Mirren's face afterwards, the insouciant swivel of her neck as she exits. And what an exit! Her red dress would have done Rita Hayworth proud.

In a 1995 profile in *The New Yorker*, Roseanne ripped actresses who complain about the dearth of good roles for women, accusing them of being out of touch with the real world (i.e., America's trailer parks). She lathered even more sarcasm on the subject speaking to Jay Leno on the *Tonight* show, saying that like some woman getting her head beat in the Midwest is really gonna go, "Well, at least Michelle Pfeiffer is getting good parts...." Roseanne's comments made for punchy sound bites; it's easy to bash movie stars as dilettantes, especially when they're not as anchored to the earth as the squatting Roseanne. But Roseanne and those who cheered her remarks are wrong. If actresses don't defend their art and demand better avenues of expression, who will? Actors aren't social workers. Their mission is not to mend the social fabric and bind personal wounds with empathy. Their difficult talent is the best thing they can bring to the table. A performance as thorny and propulsive as Helen Mirren's in the *Prime Suspect* series has a crackle that holds up even in reruns; her trim execution recalls the Humphrey Bogart of *The Maltese Falcon* and *The Big Sleep*. To create a classic portrayal is among the greatest achievements of an actor or actress. That Mirren did it on TV is a tribute to TV, a rebuke to the movies, and a reminder that the art of acting has an animal cunning that not even our self-appointed cultural commissars can tame.

the interview
By Amy Rennert

"In England, there
is a sense that
the work we do is
an art—not a way
of making money—
and that we're
carrying the
torch into the
next generation."

—HELEN MIRREN

DIDN'T KNOW WHAT TO EXPECT when I went to Manchester, England, in the summer of 1993 for my first of several conversations with Helen Mirren. It was the forty-second day of production on *Prime Suspect 3*, and the cast and crew were beginning to tire as the final days approached. A once-prosperous hospital had been transformed into police headquarters for the filming. As Mirren walked the length of the room to greet me, the tight, tired face of her character gave way to a soft, engaging expression as she introduced herself. Moments later, Tennison was back as Mirren went off to shoot another scene.

We talked later that evening. The tailored suit of the police inspector had been replaced by a long, flowing skirt and a revealing sweater, but Tennison's presence was still with us. It was as though Mirren didn't want to wander too far off character.

Months later, in Los Angeles, there was no sign of Tennison. When Mirren arrived in her '65 Ford Mustang convertible for more talk and a photo session, the tattoo on her left hand was no longer covered up by theatrical makeup. "Only criminals and

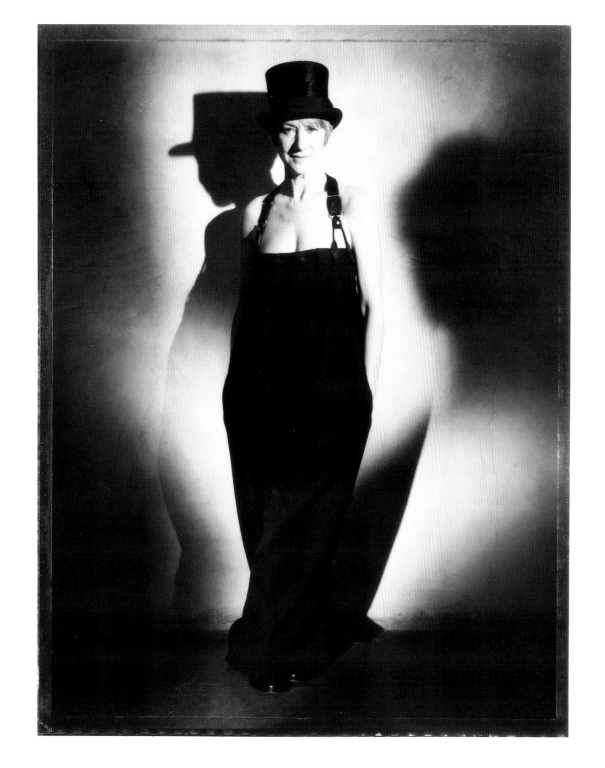

sailors had tattoos when I got this years ago," she said. "I'd show up at lavish Hollywood parties and watch people's eyes register horror when they saw it."

Our third talk took place in New York in May 1995, and this time she had an aristocratic nineteenth-century Russian woman on her mind. She was making her Broadway debut as Natalya Petrovna in Turgenev's 1850 play *A Month in the Country*.

One of Mirren's grandfathers was a tsarist colonel (he had come to Great Britain to negotiate an arms contract and was cut off from his homeland during the Russian Revolution); the other, a butcher and horse dealer in London's East End. Her father was once a violist with the London Philharmonic. Born Ilyena Lydia on July 26, 1946, the second of three children, Helen Mirren would have become a teacher had she followed her schooling. But at eighteen, on summer holiday, she tried out for the National Youth Theatre (for her audition piece, she portrayed Queen Margaret in *Henry VI*: "Even then I wanted to play strong parts"). She starred as Cleopatra in a prestigious production at the Old Vic, and soon after, she joined the Royal Shakespeare Company and went on to play most of Shakespeare's heroines. Early in her career, the *Times* of London called her "the sex queen of the RSC," and a critic claimed she was "the only Lady Macbeth who can turn you on." Over the years, she's appeared in more than 20 films, dozens of stage plays, and a number of tele-plays, moving easily among the three mediums.

She's never been married because she doesn't believe in divorce, and "I've seen too many marriages end up that way." For more than a decade, though, she has shared a home with American film director Taylor Hackford, who directed her in *White Nights* in 1985. It's her longest relationship yet and the reason she spends part of every year in the Hollywood hills

"I'm completely fascinated by the political process, but I despise politicians. I wear this pin that reads, 'Don't vote. It only encourages them.'"

—HELEN MIRREN

33

About her, critic James Wolcott wrote in *The New Yorker*, "Through Tennison, Mirren has created not only a popcult perennial worthy of Columbo's raincoat but a self-portrait of her fears, prides, and frustrations as a middle-aged actress trying to hold her own in a youth-and-beauty setup. She confronts herself and comes out the other side reaffirmed."

Long before our time together is over, I've discovered that Mirren is confident enough to do what she wants, say what she feels, and shrug when she doesn't much feel like saying anything.

Amy Rennert: Before *Prime Suspect*, you were known in this country primarily for playing sexually voracious characters in your film roles. How eager were you to portray Detective Chief Inspector Jane Tennison?

Helen Mirren: This is a role I have been waiting for. Certain roles are exactly right. I'm exactly the right age and the right mentality—I don't have to pretend to be anything other than what I am. Actresses complain about there not being enough strong roles for women. This is the kind of role they are seeking.

Rennert: You've done three *Prime Suspect* series and three *Prime Suspect* movies for television. Any worries about being typecast?

Mirren: There's a danger in coming back to character roles because you can get stuck with them. They kind of wrap you in their octopuslike arms, and you can't struggle free. I know that sounds like actor talk, but it's true. This is the first time I've done someone more than once—I've always deliberately avoided that—but Jane really is a wonderful contemporary character. You only have to look at the material you usually watch on TV and in cinema to realize how little good work there is.

Rennert: Will you continue to return to *Prime Suspect* as long as there are good scripts?

Mirren: I think I'm going to do one more, probably a four-hour series, and that will be the last one.

Rennert: You will make millions of fans on both sides of the Atlantic unhappy if you and Tennison part company.

Mirren: [Laughs] But it's like a good meal. People say, "I never want this to end," but actually they do. If it went on and on, it would be unhealthy. The wonderful advantage for me is that *Prime Suspect* hasn't been a weekly series, and that's why I have gone on longer than I thought I would.

Rennert: Tennison isn't a completely likable character, but audiences root for her. How would you describe her?

Mirren: She is a driven, obsessive, vulnerable, unpleasantly egotistical, and confused woman. But she is damn good at what she does, and totally dedicated. I also see her completely participating in life. She's very much alive.

Rennert: Do you like her?

Mirren: Yes and no. I enjoy disliking her. She isn't always a nice person. She can be selfish and driven. Those aspects are actually quite attractive in that they are forceful and dramatic. We're accustomed to seeing neurotic or hysterical women characters—victims—but we rarely see a woman whose faults are directly related to her strengths. The only way to change the perception that women have to be consistently perfect is to show that we're not. I know that it is important to project an attractive image, but male actors have been allowed the freedom to play a broad range of character types and have us care about them. It's time women claimed that right for themselves. I hope this is a turning point in the way people view female characters.

Rennert: If it were up to many of us in the audience, it would be. But are male producers and directors ready to embrace those traits in women?

Mirren: Women want power as much as any man, maybe more. They want to make their own decisions. I think men are increasingly accepting women as successful and feminine, but it's amazing how slow that process is. I keep thinking, "It's about to happen. It's going to happen now, because this has happened or that has happened. Surely the dam is going to break."

Rennert: Do you believe film, theater, and television play a major part in speeding up the social process?

Mirren: I do. I get a big response from women in many different professions who like that *Prime Suspect* is political without being propagandist. It just shows the world the way it is. And I'm glad that my character has inspired some women to be more confident and optimistic. But I think getting women into politics as quickly as possible is what's needed most, because there they have tremendous visibility. I've always said that Mrs. Thatcher was one of my great heroines; but whenever I say that, especially in England, I have to immediately disassociate myself from her politics, which I loathed. Her politics actually drove me out of England. I found them that repulsive.

Rennert: What about them was so repulsive?

Mirren: England became too much like America. In the United States, an "I've got to get it, I've got to have it" attitude makes sense. But in England that is not our tradition, and with Thatcher in power, I saw the English taking on the least attractive elements of American life and capitalism. They became very ugly people.

Rennert: Have things improved under Prime Minister John Major?

Mirren: It's not so much that Mrs. Thatcher is gone but that the false economic bubble has burst, and everybody has fallen into the shit. People are much nicer when they're in the shit than when they are floating in a fantasy, a selfish, greedy world.

"Women in many different professions like that Prime Suspect is political without being propagandist. It just shows the world the way it is."

—HELEN MIRREN

Rennert: What's your opinion of Major?

Mirren: Well, this is terrible: I can't separate Major from his voice. He's got the most unfortunate voice, a particular kind of accent. In England you're judged completely by your voice, and he's got this really awful, lower-middle-class voice. I'm not a snob—I come from the lower-middle-class myself—but he should have worked on it. That said, in a class-ridden society like ours, I have to have a soft spot for someone whose father was a circus performer and who's now the head of his country. But I hate his politics. I wouldn't be surprised if the liberal democrats start coming into their own now.

Rennert: How closely do you follow political news in England, and how active are you in politics?

Mirren: I am completely fascinated by the political process, but I despise politicians. I wear this pin that reads, "Don't vote. It only encourages them." [Laughs] In order to be a politician, you have to be a hypocrite, a liar, and basically a despiser of humanity. You never see politicians kissing babies or being nice to old people after they're elected. They only do these things when they're campaigning. That they can manipulate people so easily means they must despise them.

Rennert: If you loathed Margaret Thatcher's politics so much, how could she be such a heroine for you?

Mirren: It's wonderful if a little five- or six-year-old girl switches on the television and says, "Mummy, who's that?" and the mum says, "That's the prime minister of England." A little girl doesn't know left from right. She doesn't know from socialism or right-wing capitalism. All she sees is that a woman is the prime minister of her country. When I was growing up, I never knew such a thing was even remotely possible.

Rennert: Something must have told you it was possible to

become an actress. Was it family influence?

Mirren: No. [Pause] Well, maybe. My father's Russian, and my family name is Mironoff. Several years ago I opened the paper to read that the Laurence Olivier of Russia had died, and that his family name was Mironoff. So perhaps there was some distant connection.

Rennert: Could you talk a little about your early family life?

Mirren: I grew up with a brother and a sister in a small seaside town, Southend-on-Sea. It always rained. People used to go there for their summer holidays; only the British can sit on the beach in the rain, a sight I've seen many times in Southend. The town was like the Coney Island of London, only not quite as wild. It's very working-class, or lower-income, as you call it in America.

I was incredibly foolish as a child, always having fantasies, never very practical.

Rennert: And what did you dream for yourself?

Mirren: I wanted to be an actress from a very early age. I didn't quite know why, but I used to lie in my bed looking out the window at night at a particular configuration of stars, and I would see this huge letter A in the sky. It was enormous, and it was the last thing I would see before going to sleep. For me, it represented Acting, and it represented America. That was another dream, that I would go to America one day.

Rennert: What is it that drove you to be an actress?

Mirren: My desire really came from Shakespeare. I found his stories so much more interesting than the Rock Hudson and Doris Day movies that would come to my little town.

Rennert: In this country, we're not teaching Shakespeare much in the schools. Are we in danger of losing our ability to appreciate serious drama as a result?

Mirren: I've always thought that Shakespeare shouldn't be

taught in schools. You should see the plays completely fresh, without knowing what happens. Can you imagine! You don't know that Ophelia goes mad, you don't know that Hamlet is going to die—the impact of watching that play would be enormous. To this day, I can't read Shakespeare. I find it incredibly difficult.

Rennert: You've portrayed all the great Shakespearean women—Ophelia, Lady Macbeth, Cleopatra. Do you want to return to Shakespeare?

Mirren: Some of the roles I could do again. It's good to go back to a role because there's so much in Shakespeare, and you never get it right. [Laughs] But there are very few good Shakespearean roles for women my age, and so many fabulous male roles. There's such inequity.

Rennert: The same can be said for the movies and television. There aren't many leading roles for women your age. That's why Tennison is such a breakthrough character. It's wonderful—and very unusual—to see a beautiful, fortysomething woman on the screen in such a major role. Your character doesn't seem afraid to show her age.

Mirren: With Tennison, you see everything. If you don't like it, too bad. It's so much better to think like that. It's the advantage that male actors have—they don't have to bother with mascara and worry so much about how they look. It's disappointing to me that so many American actresses are obsessed with good looks. They feel they have to work out in some gym for ten hours a day if they're going to do a nude scene. They believe they have to be perfect. I mean, please. Life's too short.

Rennert: The truth is most American actresses don't do their own nude scenes. They use body doubles. But in all your roles, you seem completely comfortable in your body.

"The only way to change the percep-tion that women have to be perfect is to show we're not."

—HELEN MIRREN

Mirren: Agewise, you have to move on. As much as I admire women such as Cher and Jane Fonda for taking control of their lives, this obsession with looks has gotten out of control. I think we have to say, "Yes, we do get older" because we do. And I don't mind saying how it is, if you know what I mean. The amazing thing is that audiences don't mind, either. Audiences are constantly underestimated and insulted by American producers.

Rennert: It sounds as if both you and your character have come up against authority figures who are a little out of touch with the real world.

Mirren: Yes. Tennison is fighting a world that has its rules. You cannot flank, and you can't sail off directly into the wind. You will only get blown back. So you have to tack against the wind, and you have to be very, very clever. Women want to be as much like men as possible, because if they look obviously different, they get a lot of flak. I know it sounds trivial, but cutting my hair short for the role was the most difficult preparation. With each snip I got more into character. For some reason, there's this idea that powerful, intelligent women have to have short hair. Look at the clothes that policewomen wear—very tailored dark suits and ties.

Rennert: They're supposed to fit into a masculine world, but not too much, because that has other traps.

Mirren: Right. In many ways, we've underplayed how much women in powerful roles have to give up. It's incredibly difficult for them. In England a woman was sacked from her job for being too bossy. For being too bossy! She was the head of a health organization, and her patients loved her. They fought for her because they said her only interest was to give them good care. But the bureaucracy hated her because she had to be extremely aggressive with her colleagues in order to provide that good care.

Rennert: Several years ago, an English survey indicated that 90

"So many American actresses are obsessed with good looks. They feel they have to work out in some gym for ten hours a day if they are going to do a nude scene. I mean, please. Life's too short."

—HELEN MIRREN

percent of those polled would choose to have a male detective investigate if one of their loved ones were murdered. Do you think *Prime Suspect* might affect the results in a new poll?

Mirren: Definitely.

Rennert: Would you rather have a male or female detective assigned to a case?

Mirren: Now, I would say I wouldn't mind either way. Ten years ago I used to think of the police as the enemy. I had absolutely no confidence in them, male or female. And I've always been nervous around them; whenever one was following me, I'd get sweaty palms. But doing the series has given me more respect for the cops—an informed kind of respect, not blind admiration.

Rennert: How have the police responded to the series?

Mirren: They like it. The police love to see themselves on television—when the camera is turned on them, they are on their best behavior. What they don't like to see is a real-life documentary that's been secretly filmed.

Rennert: Something like the Rodney King videotaped beating or other police exposé tapes. Still, I'm a bit surprised that they enjoy watching the series, since the cops on *Prime Suspect* are not always portrayed in a favorable light. Corruption and cover-ups are often part of the story.

Mirren: One of the great things about the series is that it is fairly critical of the police. The biggest response I've had is from people in the streets, often young black guys, who say, "Hey, you're that lady cop. Keep up the good work. It's fab!"

Rennert: What has changed now that the format is a two-hour movie and creator Lynda La Plante is not involved?

Mirren: With the three miniseries, we really had time to explore the texture of the characters and do wonderful character development. You aren't really able to do that in the two-hour format.

Lynda created such an extraordinary life force—an amazing invention. But I do think there has been great consciousness of not shifting the terrain and continuing in a way that is faithful to her original creation.

Rennert: You've had a very busy two years. In addition to making the *Prime Suspect* movies, you starred in *A Month in the Country,* first in England and then on Broadway. What attracted you to Turgenev's play and Natalya Petrovna?

Mirren: The play is about love and the foolishness it creates, the way people mislead themselves when they're in love, how all judgment goes out the window. It is about the tormented side of love, and it's also a wonderful comedy. Natalya's such an extraordinary character, ultimately foolish and out of control. There's always something going on inside Natalya—her mind is in a tempest or confusion. She has so many different levels and layers. I constantly go back to the text for more clues to her.

Rennert: When do you do that?

Mirren: All the time, I study it. I even sit and read it when I'm offstage during the performance. It's not to remind myself of the lines. It's funny about a spoken line and a written one: You're saying exactly the same words, but there's a very different resonance on the page. It's difficult to describe. It seems to have a mystery on the page that it doesn't necessarily have in your mouth. I'm always trying to get back to the mystery of what's behind the words on the page. I can't really articulate this very well. [Pause] I'm constantly trying to find other psychological interpretations, which then push the line out of the mouth in a different way. I keep trying to get back to Turgenev's imagined Natalya Petrovna as opposed to mine, and I constantly refind her.

Rennert: Can you feel the response of the audience each night?

Mirren: Ah! Yes, you feel it within the first three minutes. One

"A line seems to have a mystery on the page that it doesn't necessarily have in your mouth. I'm always trying to get back to the mystery of what's behind the words on the page."

—HELEN MIRREN

night, for instance, was a special gay singles night, and it was the most wonderful audience. They were so responsive. I wish we could have gay singles night every night. [Laughs]

Rennert: Before taking on the play, you were in the film *The Madness of King George*. How did that role come about?

Mirren: Yes, *George* just blessedly and wonderfully came along, and I jumped at it. On the page it wasn't the most exciting role; I was amazed when I was nominated for an Oscar. That was incomprehensible, but I loved that the film was true to history.

Rennert: It may not have been a large role, but I felt it was a flawless performance. I was very moved by the character's loyalty to the king and their relationship.

Mirren: I read as much as I could about her and tried to find out, without being too literal, what I felt she was. She was an absolutely sweet woman, and charming. And, as you say, she was incredibly loyal. She was a princess from a small kingdom somewhere in the middle of Germany. It was an arranged marriage—they hadn't even met when they married. It was a marriage made in heaven because they absolutely adored each other. They slept together every night and that's unheard of even today, for the royal family to sleep together. But they simply never wanted to be apart. They shared everything. I thought the mark of her character was when she first set foot in England at age seventeen or eighteen and refused to ever speak German again. She said, "This is my country now, and they speak English here." She had an enormous sense of duty. They both did, and that is why the Prince Regent devastated both of them. He went as far in the other direction as possible.

Rennert: You went as far in another direction as possible with some of your previous films. What attracted you to *The Cook, the Thief, His Wife and Her Lover*?

"Director Peter Greenaway is brilliant at getting right into your subconscious in a way that has a very deep effect on you but is not destructive."

—HELEN MIRREN

Mirren: Well, Peter Greenaway, the director, is a wonderful writer. I kept the script to that film because it reads like literature, and everything that happens in the film is described on the pages of the script. Usually with scripts, you take a thick black marker and cross out all the stage directions so that you can get right to the dialogue. The stage directions are often misleading or silly or restricting in some way, but with Peter it's exactly the opposite, because the stage directions are so vivid and wonderful.

Rennert: But the film wasn't universally well received. Many people were so disturbed by it they walked out—

Mirren: And I couldn't understand what they were talking about, because Peter is brilliant at getting into your subconscious in a way that has a very deep effect on you but is not destructive.

Rennert: What sort of films would you consider destructive?

Mirren: Films like *Total Recall*, for instance. There's a scene in which "our hero" is on a crowded escalator and he grabs a dead body to protect himself against being shot. One by one, people are killed. I watched and I thought, "I can't believe I'm seeing what I'm seeing." It was so soulless. At least *The Cook, the Thief* or *Henry: Portrait of a Serial Killer*, an intensely violent film, seriously put you off any kind of violence. In *Henry*, death is made to look horrible and disgusting.

Rennert: More and more people are becoming convinced that violence in the media contributes to violence in the streets. What do you think?

Mirren: I don't mind violence on television or in movies if they show it how it is. But I have a huge problem with movies and TV programs that are just bang-bang.

Rennert: In this country, onscreen violence has gotten so out of control that the government is threatening to take steps if the television industry doesn't monitor itself. How bad is the situation on English TV?

Mirren: We have a different form of violence. I was just watching a trailer for one upstairs. It was about predators eating each other. [Laughs] They love those in England. Anything that has to do with something eating something else. I saw one with this sweet little fish swimming about while other animals hid, disguising themselves until they could pounce. Here's this sweet little thing just swimming along, and out of the sand rises this huge great fish. Ca-runch! Awful! [Laughs] It's awful.

Rennert: Well, our taste for some things may differ, but American and English viewers alike seem to agree that *Prime Suspect* is great television. The ratings have been sky-high in both countries. Do you get a similar response from fans?

Mirren: When we first did the series, we didn't know if it was going to fly in America; we thought maybe it was too English. But the reaction has been similar—the only noticeable difference is that American audiences are much more vocal and more likely to tell you exactly what they think. The English are reserved.

Rennert: Do you find that the two countries have different creative styles as well?

Mirren: Yes. There's no sense in England of being a television actor or a film actor or a theater actor—we don't limit ourselves to one particular discipline. We travel among the three, and we have much more fun. I like the touring, the backstage jokes, the camaraderie, the laughing, the despair, the drunken evenings in the bar. We're very lucky in England, even though we work much more often for much less money.

Rennert: *The Remains of the Day* and *The Crying Game* are two English movies that were critical and commercial successes. But are there very many opportunities to work in film in England?

Mirren: No. The film market doesn't exist. There's no business.

In a way it's to the advantage of filmmaking, because where the business doesn't exist, you get to be more idiosyncratic. Europeans have never quite grasped the idea of movies as a commodity. They've always insisted on seeing movies as an art form, really.

Rennert: Hollywood would have a difficult time relating to that.

Mirren: I love Hollywood—it is such a whore. It just goes with the flow, the wind, the market. It never has a hidden agenda. But I've never been all that attracted to being an American movie star. I prefer to be an English actor.

Rennert: What's the difference?

Mirren: Hollywood is very much about manipulation and hype. In England there is a sense of the culture, a sense that the work we do is an art, not a way of making money, and that we're carrying the torch into the next generation.

Rennert: For several years you've been dividing your time between the two countries. Do you ever think of yourself as American?

Mirren: No. I have enormous respect for America. I've lived here a lot and I have a great love for the country. But I will never be an American because I have a return ticket. A woman who has just run across the border from Tijuana, a woman who has been in the country for only five hours, is already more American than I will ever be because she is there without options, without a return ticket. She understands that it's a do-or-die situation.

Rennert: How does moving back and forth between the two countries affect you?

Mirren: It's been great. They are two distinct cultures that share the language. I've always enjoyed traveling between cultures, and I find they provide a good balance. America's been very good for me. My sort of English thing has been quite liberated by living in America.

> "I love Hollywood—it is such a whore. It just goes with the flow, the wind, the market."
>
> —HELEN MIRREN

Rennert: I think you're going to have to explain that one.

Mirren: In England we all mock the Americans' ability to talk about themselves, to spew out all this stuff. We rather despise that in England, but I've learned it has tremendous value if it's contained. Now I can confront things I couldn't. I don't have to be in control of my emotions all the time. I can show despair, disappointment, ambition—all things you mustn't show in England. You've got to be cool, basically. Constantly cool. And America's taught me to be uncool.

by tom shales

S ERIAL KILLER ON THE LOOSE, women disappearing, police confounded. That may sound like the plot of a thousand TV movies, but nothing about *Prime Suspect* is much less than extraordinary.

The impeccably gritty drama is much less about the crimes than about the criminal, and much less about the criminal than about the top cop in pursuit: Detective Chief Inspector Tennison. Tennison's first name is Jane. Not only must she catch the killer, she must also prove herself to the doubting old-boy network of the London police department, where the idea of a woman running an investigation is new and wildly unpopular.

The blunt-speaking *Prime Suspect* is totally atypical of the usual quaint *Mystery!* fare and really should have been offered as a *Masterpiece Theatre*. Is it that good? It's better.

Helen Mirren is the main reason. Her portrayal of Tennison is ice-hard but not ice-cold, a brilliant parlay of backbone and heart. Mirren doesn't take a breath or blink an eye that isn't in character; everything contributes to a portrait of a cool, canny dynamo who knows she can't allow herself any signs of weakness or indecision. The men are watching and waiting for her to

WAITING FOR JUSTICE

Producer: Don Leaver   Director: Chris Menaul   Writer: Lynda La Plante

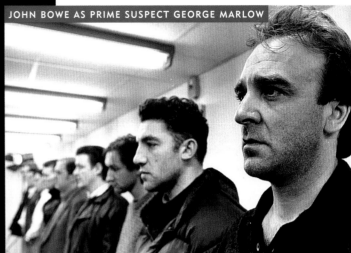

"Prime Suspect reinvents both the psychological thriller and the police procedural, not merely by making the detective a woman (Agatha Christie already did that), but by allowing her to triumph over the misogyny that's both outside and within the law."

—AMY TAUBIN
THE VILLAGE VOICE

53

JOHN BOWE
GEORGE MARLOW

Half British and half American, John Bowe has acted on both sides of the Atlantic, most notably as Le Bret in *Cyrano de Bergerac* in Los Angeles, New York, and Washington, DC. He performed in British and world tours of *The Royal Hunt of the Sun*, *Pilgrim*, and *Henry V*; in *Saint Joan* at the Old Vic; as Iago in *Othello* with the New Shakespeare Company; and in a wide variety of roles in his seven years with the Royal Shakespeare Company. He's been in two British-made films and several television shows. After *Prime Suspect*, he took a major part in a daytime soap on Granada Television, *Families*.

bend, to crack, even to crease a little.

To complicate the case, Tennison (almost an anagram of "tension") is following in the footsteps of a veteran cop whose sudden death by heart attack has greatly bereaved "the lads" on the force. She doesn't just follow in those footsteps, however; she muddies them. It seems the officer may have been accepting sexual favors from a prostitute who was one of the victims.

While the investigation runs into plenty of obstacles and detours, Tennison's biggest problems are in the police station itself, where diehards oppose her and even attempt sabotage. Most rabid of the lot is the embittered misogynist Bill Otley (Tom Bell), but the filmmakers try to understand him, not just use him as a stock villain.

Both the executive producer and the writer of *Prime Suspect* are women: producer Sally Head and novelist Lynda La Plante. By no means have they made this a feminist tract. It isn't the tireless saintly female against the nasty beastly men, partly because Tennison herself is anything but perfect. She smokes, she swears, she is sometimes strident and tactless. When she insists on grilling the grieving father of a slain girl, an officer pleads with her, "Let the man cry; he's heartbroken." In an autopsy room, it's the male cop who gets nauseated, not her. Tennison brings her obsession with the case home, driving housemate Peter (Tom Wilkins) away. One's affection for her may waver, but never one's respect.

Another refreshing thing about the drama is its depiction of the title character. This prime suspect is no (outwardly) demonic figure but instead a puppy-faced forty-year-old named George Marlow (John Bowe), who sings "You'll Never Walk Alone" with his dear old mum when visiting her at a rest home. Such a nice chap, and yet Tennison feels certain he goes around raping and

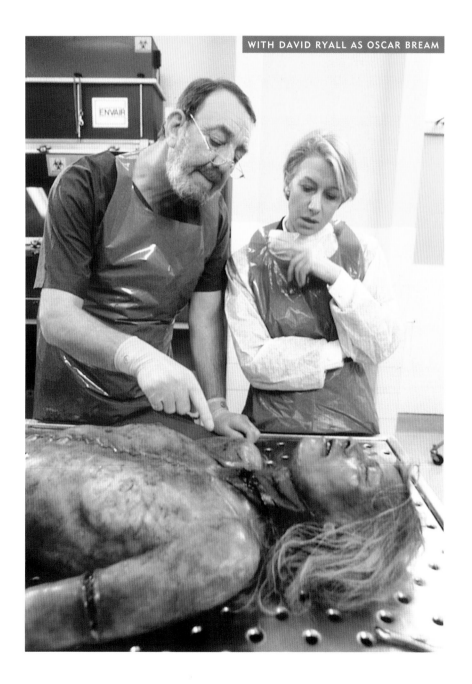

Ralph Fiennes is considered one of the finest young actors working today. So it says something about the quality of the acting in *Prime Suspect* that in his one scene—a strong and moving one, in which he learns the gruesome circumstances of his girlfriend's death—he doesn't blow everyone else out of the water.

Since his work in *Prime Suspect*, of course, Fiennes has played two acclaimed film roles: the sadistic Nazi commandant Amon Goeth in Steven Spielberg's *Schindler's List*, which brought him an Oscar nomination, and the patrician college professor Charles Van Doren in Robert Redford's *Quiz Show*.

Fiennes (his name is pronounced Rafe Fines, in the Old English manner) grew up in rural Suffolk, England, although his father, a landscape photographer, ➤

RALPH FIENNES
MICHAEL

◄ moved the family all over the United Kingdom. His mother was a writer and painter. Young Ralph had planned to become an artist as well; instead, in 1982, he auditioned successfully for the Royal Academy of Dramatic Art. Five years later, he joined the Royal Shakespeare Company and was well reviewed in a number of classic roles. But it was his magnetic T.E. Lawrence in a 1992 TV movie called *A Dangerous Man* that drew Spielberg's attention.

"Helen constantly encourages people to give and go further than they would have done. You get a lot braver once you've worked with her."

—RICHARD HAWLEY
(DET. INSP. RICHARD HASKONS)

Zoe Wanamaker would never have become a British actress if not for the Hollywood blacklist. Born in New York, she is the daughter of the late American actor-director Sam Wanamaker, who moved his family to England when he could no longer get work in Hollywood during the HUAC-haunted fifties.

Wanamaker worked steadily in acting from college on, in repertory, TV drama-documentaries, "whatever came along." She received a Tony nomination for her work in *Piaf* and another for Joe Orton's *Loot*. Wanamaker considers herself "rather too English" for life in the US. American audiences, though, have seen her in *Paradise Postponed* on PBS and in Bob Hoskins' directorial debut, *The Raggedy Rawney*, among other films.

ZOE WANAMAKER
MOYRA HENSON

murdering. As Marlow, John Bowe is criminally good. As his brittle, battle-scarred, common-law wife, Moyra, Zoe Wanamaker looks daggers and breathes fire. When Moyra and Jane Tennison face each other in the final installment, it's a riveting showdown, a clichéd situation turned inside out and made new again.

What makes *Prime Suspect* so gripping is that it's not really about crime or cops, it's about the best and worst in human beings and the way each reveals itself. The film defies the stereotype of public TV programming. It isn't stiff, it isn't stuffy. It's sensational, and it's mostly Mirren's triumph.

"Tennison is nearly all repression, which is what, in Mirren's skilled hands, makes her so fascinating: Her emotions don't come at us, we have to lean in and pay attention to grasp her." —DIANE WERTS NEW YORK NEWSDAY

PRIME SUSPECT 2

by amy taubin

TRUCTURED MUCH LIKE THE initial series, *Prime Suspect 2* is a police procedural in which the principal dramatic conflict is not between the detective and the murderer, but between Jane Tennison and her fellow workers—one of them her boss, the other a subordinate. The boss, Chief Superintendent Michael Kernan (John Benfield), knows how good she is but nevertheless sells her out, believing her advancement will be detrimental to his own. And if in the first series her most adversarial subordinate was also the most virulent woman-hater (an unforgettable performance by Tom Bell), here the person most resistant to her authority is also the person who should be most in sync with her

Producer: Paul Marcus Director: John Strickland Writer: Allan Cubitt

He's appeared in plays ranging from *Macbeth* and *Twelfth Night* to *The Duchess of Malfi* and *She Stoops to Conquer.* But John Benfield's career has been largely in television. (After *Prime Suspect*, he worked on a more traditional mystery, *Maigret*, in Budapest.) It may mean more to British viewers than American ones that he appeared in three *Eurocop*s films. His other television appearances have been in both comedies and dramas, including classics such as *The Beggar's Opera, The Winter's Tale, Titus Andronicus,* and *Henry VI*, parts 1, 2, and 3.

JOHN BENFIELD
CHIEF SUPT. MICHAEL KERNAN

because, as the token black officer, Detective Sergeant Robert Oswalde (Colin Salmon) is as much an outsider as she is.

Prime Suspect 2 opens with Tennison interviewing an accused rapist, whose stony black face is the first image we see in the film—an unmistakable indication that this time around, racism is going to be as much of an attention-grabber as sexism. As it turns out, it's a simulated interrogation, with Detective Oswalde playing the rapist. But something in the exchange has struck a real emotional chord, and Tennison and Oswalde wind up in bed. Her motivation has as much to do with issues of power as libido. Tennison wants to be allowed the kind of casual sex that men assume is part of the program when they go to out-of-town conferences. What's more, playacting with Oswalde has turned her on not merely because he's an attractive man, but because he's an attractive black man. "What was it you said about white women wanting it rough?" she asks, in a flat-footed attempt at flirtation. "That wasn't me," he replies angrily. "I just don't like being treated like some black stud." "That's in your head," she answers testily, but her expression suggests otherwise, that she's recognized some hidden strain of racism in herself, some myth of black sexuality churning at the edge of consciousness. After all, it's hardly an accident that Oswalde was chosen to impersonate the rapist, that rape and racism were so neatly packaged that the connection went unnoted by everyone except Oswalde.

What at first seems like a casual encounter is, in fact, the opening gambit in the struggle over race, sex, and power that is spun out over the entire series. The tryst is broken short by a telephone call: The body of a young black woman has been discovered in an Afro-Caribbean neighborhood, and Tennison is to head the investigation. Without consulting her, Kernan drafts Oswalde (who works in a different precinct) to be part of the

COLIN SALMON
DET. SGT. ROBERT OSWALDE

Colin Salmon's background is mixed: English mother, Jamaican father, Ghanaian birth father. He grew up near Cambridge. Later, he took his trumpet to London and began "busking" on street corners, the most promising of which was outside a fringe theater called The Tricycle. Two of the actors arranged a permanent spot (as busker) for him; a few years later, after he had taken drama lessons, the theater cast him in a musical about Billie Holiday titled *All or Nothing at All*.

As with many young British actors, his stage work has ranged from fringe and avant-garde works to European tours (*Porgy and Bess*) and West End productions (*Buddy*). He had never worked in television before his star-making appearance in *Prime Suspect*.

team. But Tennison is furious: In the confusion of personal and professional relationships, she feels that Oswalde has power over her. She's angry at herself for having committed a potentially career-threatening indiscretion, but she takes it out on him by confining him to menial tasks—treating the token black man exactly as she, the token woman, was treated on her way up.

Race is on everybody's mind. There's the mother of the murdered girl, brought in to identify her daughter's body. She's white, her husband was black; her daughter ran away after he died. She wants Oswalde to explain what happened. Was it her fault because she was involved in a mixed marriage? There's the middle-class black family whose fragile son, Tony, is a prime suspect—they accuse Oswalde of being a "coconut" and projecting his own anxieties on them.

While racism supersedes sexism in *Prime Suspect 2*, Tennison is still the motor and the reason the series is so compelling. In the context of American TV (and film), it's incredible that she's so flawed, so much a bundle of compensations. And how could she be otherwise when the law she's bound to uphold is such a mess? In the third episode, there's a repellent tour de force that cuts between Tennison coaxing a deathbed confession out of her prime suspect (stroking his fingers, pretending to care about the state of his soul) and Oswalde browbeating the hysterical Tony. Afterward, Tennison goes into the bathroom and scrubs her hands, as if to wash away not only the criminal's touch but the hypocrisy of her method. She looks in the mirror long enough for us to know she doesn't like what she sees, that she loathes what she has to do to win. It goes without saying that Tennison solves the murder, but unlike in the first series, there's no uplift, only the confusion of guilt, privilege, and responsibility, and the weight of the glass ceiling pressing on her head.

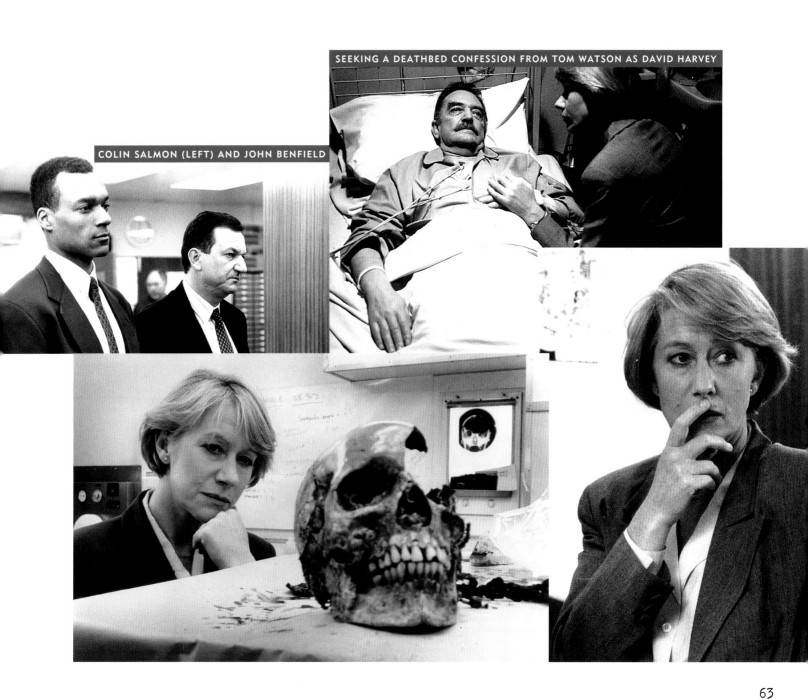

COLIN SALMON (LEFT) AND JOHN BENFIELD

SEEKING A DEATHBED CONFESSION FROM TOM WATSON AS DAVID HARVEY

PRIME SUSPECT 3

by tom shales

TOM BELL RETURNS AS TENNISON'S NEMESIS BILL OT

VEN IF ALL THE OTHER ACTORS in it were terrible, it would be worth watching *Prime Suspect 3* just to see Helen Mirren return in the role of Detective Chief Inspector Jane Tennison. She still seems fresh in it; she's still exploring, still discovering. It's hard to remember a better fit between actor and role. Mirren makes Tennison a thoroughly fascinating figure.

Anyone who thought the first two *Prime Suspect*s a bit dark and forbidding should be warned that the third miniseries is the

Producer: Paul Marcus   Director: David Drury   Writer: Lynda La Plante

DAVID THEWLIS AS JIMMY JACKSON

PETER CAPALDI AS VERA REYNOLDS

"Tom Bell's hard-assed cop is a miniature of under-playing, especially in his gradual rapprochement with his female boss. As the pimp (and prime suspect), David Thewlis is a magnetic study in sleaze. Peter Capaldi makes a sad, touching transsexual. But it's still Mirren's show."

—VARIETY

It's a measure of the way Tom Bell inhabits a role that viewers of *Prime Suspect* may not think they've seen him in any other PBS series, until they learn that—among many, many other television appearances—he was in *Reilly, Ace of Spies*. Then, after a beat or two, no more, most viewers of that popular show will know: "Ah! Felix Dzerzhinsky."

Bell left school in the Morecambe area of England to join a local repertory company at the age of fifteen. He made his name in the early sixties as the brooding young writer in the acclaimed film *The L-Shaped Room*, and he has appeared in a number of British movies since then. Most recently, he was seen by American audiences in *The Kray Twins* and *Prospero's Books*.

In television, he's been in productions such as *Sons and Lovers* and *Hedda Gabler*. On stage, he appeared in *Travesties* with the Royal Shakespeare Company and played opposite Ian McKellen in *Bent*. He claims he's not interested in doing the classics and isn't much drawn by the stimulus of a live audience. He says, "My talent is for film acting; that's where I feel at home."

grimmest yet. Tennison has been transferred to the vice squad and promptly sets to work solving the murder of a young male prostitute (a "rent boy," as British jargon puts it) with links to a gang of pedophiles. Her investigation takes her into the dankest corners of the sexual twilight world and also into the upper echelons of department ranks. Tennison wouldn't be Tennison if she weren't stepping on toes willy-nilly and risking all in the relentless pursuit of duty.

Prime Suspect 3 is grippingly suspenseful virtually from the get-go. Although Tennison has slain most of the male chauvinist dragons with whom she's come into contact, she is reunited in the first installment with an old intimidating nemesis: Tom Bell as Detective Sergeant Bill Otley. Part of the suspense as the serial goes along is trying to figure out who among her male colleagues is leaking information to higher-ups as Tennison goes about her business.

The prime suspect in the murder of seventeen-year-old Colin Jenkins (Greg Saunders) seems clear early on. Jimmy Jackson (played to mealy-mouthed perfection by David Thewlis) is a pimp, a whore, and a pornographer, plus God knows what else. But then another suspect emerges, Edward Parker-Jones (Ciaran Hinds), who runs a youth center designed to shelter boys from the very evils to which he may be exposing them.

Other denizens of the deep whom Tennison encounters include actor Peter Capaldi as Vera Reynolds, a perpetually frightened transsexual who opens the serial singing "Falling in Love Again" à la Marlene Dietrich at a supposedly posh gay bar. As she sings, fire is consuming the apartment in which young Jenkins lies.

Prime Suspect 3 takes one into a world of shadowy sex; at times, the "rent boys" seem sad descendants of the urchins Charles Dickens wrote about in the nineteenth century. In a way,

PEARCE QUIGLEY AS RED

> "When Mirren stalks the halls, she's not self-conscious like Murphy Brown, or dogmatic like Mary Beth Lacey; she's just a beat-up detective having a bad day."
>
> —SUSAN STEWART
> DETROIT FREE PRESS

TOM BELL WITH RICHARD CADMAN AS STREET URCHIN ALAN THORPE

PETER CAPALDI
VERA REYNOLDS

As the transsexual nightclub singer in whose apartment police discover the body of a murdered "rent boy," Peter Capaldi looks nothing like the Scots hotel keeper with whom Peter Riegert wanted to exchange lives in the Bill Forsyth film *Local Hero*. Ironically, Capaldi got very little work after that job. "There wasn't much demand for inexperienced 23-year-old Scottish actors at the time," he says. Capaldi even thought of giving up acting, then decided "it's a million times better than a lot of jobs."

He's since found work in other films, such as *Dangerous Liaisons* and *Selling Hitler*. His television credits include *The Cloning of Joanna May, Titmus Regained*, and *Poirot*.

JOHN BENFIELD (LEFT) WITH TERRENCE HARDIMAN
COMMANDER CHISWICK

TOM BELL (AS BILL OTLEY) ENLISTS THE AID OF THE RENT BOYS

PETER CAPALDI AS VERA REYNOLDS ONSTAGE

When David Thewlis signed on for *Prime Suspect 3*, he was known by audiences—if he was remembered at all—for a small role in Mike Leigh's charming 1991 film *Life Is Sweet*. By the time he arrived on the set, he had starred in another film directed by Leigh, *Naked*—and won best actor awards in Britain, the US, and Cannes.

Thewlis grew up in working-class Blackpool and studied at London's Guildhall School of Music and Drama. In addition to small roles in BBC and other television productions (*The Trial*, *The Singing Detective*) and on stage (*The Sea*, *Buddy Holly at the Regal*), he played the ill-fated son of Jeremy Irons and Miranda Richardson in Louis Malle's motion picture *Damage*.

DAVID THEWLIS
JIMMY JACKSON

69

this is Oliver Twisted.

Most of the pedophilia described in the serial is homosexual. To balance the portrait of gay men, writer Lynda La Plante includes an honest, upright, non-child-molesting gay cop who "comes out" in Part 3. Even so, *Prime Suspect 3* may earn the odd distinction of offending both gay groups and the right-wingers who regularly like to attack public television.

If it seems that excessive attention is being paid to Tennison's private life—mainly, a breakup with a boyfriend—this element pays off later with a startling revelation and a disquieting resolution. Tennison carries the weight of the world on her shoulders, and even she comes within an inch of cracking now and then. Indeed, in one episode she actually weeps, but turns her back to the camera when she does it. What she keeps in firm grip is her stubborn integrity. As a cop in Manchester says to her, "I hear very good things about you. You're not scared of anything."

Prime Suspect 3 is probably better than *Prime Suspect 2* in terms of plot and atmospherics, and almost as good as the original miniseries overall. The one area where it disappoints is the ending devised by La Plante, which is not as conclusive as one would hope. Perhaps La Plante was trying to be socially portentous, telling us that even if culprits are apprehended, the tragic problems of child prostitution and pornography will not go away. Or perhaps we are to make an assumption about the fate of one character based on the lingering last shot. Still, you may feel cheated, as I did, and even find yourself thinking, "That Lynda La Plante can go take a flying leap."

Even with this shortcoming, which is minor in the long run, *Prime Suspect 3* remains one of the most absorbing, well-acted, and mercilessly nerve-wracking dramas of the season. "Sensational" would not be too strong a word.

"The second-most-memorable face in the series belongs to David Thewlis, who plays a snarling, whining, crafty pervert. As with his stellar performance in <u>Naked</u>, Thewlis gives us the wised-up, gone-wrong tones of junk Britain."

—CHRISTOPHER HITCHENS
<u>VANITY FAIR</u>

71

Sisters in crime: Helen Mirren and Lynda La Plante

the woman
behind the woman
By Marilee Strong

ITHOUT LYNDA LA PLANTE, there would be no *Prime Suspect*, and Helen Mirren would not have encountered the most memorable character of her career.

The creative force behind the series is herself a Shakespearean-trained actress. After winning a scholarship at sixteen to the Royal Academy of Dramatic Art, La Plante, now forty-nine, worked steadily on television and in the theater, including stints with the Royal Shakespeare Company and Britain's National Theatre Company. But instead of playing classical heroines as Mirren did, La Plante, with her shock of curly red hair, was stereotyped as a tart. In 1983, she gave up acting to try her hand at writing: If she could not find good roles for women, La Plante thought, she would create them.

She hit it big in the mid-1980s after penning a successful television series about a group of bank robbers' widows who themselves turn to crime—indulging, for the first time, her fascination with both powerful women and the criminal mind. Then she hit a wall of rejections. By the time she sat down to lunch in 1990 with the script editor of Britain's Granada Television, who had worked on a previous La Plante project shelved by the BBC,

"I can't stress enough how beautifully scripted I found the program. It has absolutely influenced my writing of female characters."

—STEPHEN CANNELL
TV WRITER-PRODUCER, CREATOR OF THE ROCKFORD FILES, AND AUTHOR OF THE PLAN

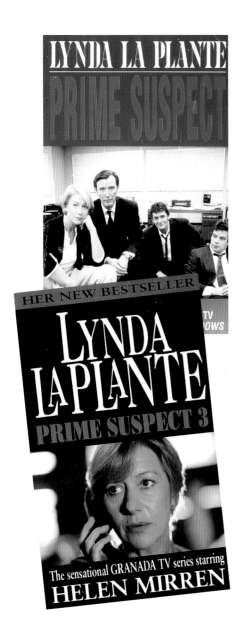

La Plante was beginning to have second thoughts about her career change. She certainly wasn't expecting the editor to tell her, "If you've got anything, I'm in a prime situation to put it forward right now."

"I sat there with my left brain working at twenty-five knots thinking, What hasn't been done?" La Plante recalls in an exuberant British accent. (She's originally from Liverpool.) "And out of my mouth came 'I'm very interested in doing a police show with a woman heading a homicide team.'" "Oh, that's good," cooed the editor. "What are you going to call it?" La Plante's mind raced again. "Prime Suspect," she heard herself say.

Granada was interested in *Prime Suspect*—so interested that La Plante had to scramble to gather enough facts to rush out a scene-by-scene description. She telephoned London's Metropolitan Police and its uppermost echelon, Scotland Yard, to ask how many high-ranking women detectives the department had. "Hmm, that's a difficult question," the spokesman said. "You mean out on the street, actually working in a station? I think we have...four."

La Plante, who gathers material for her scripts like a journalist, asked to speak to the women. When Detective Chief Inspector Jackie Malton rang her doorbell the next night, the writer knew she had found the model for her protagonist. "Whatever I was expecting, I was confronted with this energy-driven woman who was absolutely adorable," remembers La Plante. "She was sharp, she was tough, and she was very, very funny. I suddenly had in front of me the most wonderfully complex character."

Then a twenty-one-year veteran of the police force, Malton was in charge of forty-five detectives in West London, having achieved a rank equivalent to a lieutenant on an American police

"I always pushed
the dramatic
tension to the
absolute limit. I
didn't make
Tennison an icon.
She is very
flawed."

—LYNDA LA PLANTE

75

force. Her rise, however, was fraught with discrimination and brutal sexist humor. Her own detectives withheld information from her on investigations. When called to a murder scene, they raced to the car, slamming the door on her if necessary to keep her from the radio seat normally reserved for the senior officer. An officer once told her she needed to take fingerprints from a corpse. What he didn't tell her—and found hysterically funny—was that rigor mortis would cause the corpse's hand to clamp over hers, and she'd be unable to release its grip. When Harrod's department store was bombed, she was horrified to hear a male officer joke about the dead policewoman whose clothes had been blown off by the force of the blast. "There were so many things the men dealt with through humor," says La Plante. "But she had no one to bounce her feelings off."

La Plante shadowed Malton for months, interviewing killers, watching autopsies, and forming, in her own mind, the character of Jane Tennison. When Malton rang La Plante's doorbell that first night, she had been wearing jeans and a bomber jacket. But at work, she wore her "uniform": a smart tailored suit, never pants, nothing provocative. "When we walked into the police station, I saw another person take over—this chameleon woman of such strength and resources, and such pain sometimes," says La Plante. There, Malton was "ma'am." She never touched the men who worked for her; even to rest an arm around one of them would be considered a sexual statement. And she never, ever allowed herself to show her emotions at work.

"I'm supposed to be the leader," she told La Plante. "If I crack, their confidence in me waivers." When an eighteen-month-old child was raped and murdered, a young male officer cried in Malton's arms. "Don't let anybody know I broke down," he begged her. "Nobody's going to know," she promised. Only later,

The real-life model for Tennison: Detective Chief Inspector Jackie Malton

in the privacy of her office, did she let her own tears flow.

La Plante strove for that complex mix of toughness and tenderness in her fictional detective. DCI Tennison is a long way from Agatha Christie's eccentric Miss Marple, or the gentle Jessica Fletcher of *Murder, She Wrote*. Even *Cagney & Lacey*—light-years from Angie Dickinson's sexpot *Policewoman*—dumped one of its original stars because she was deemed too hard and too unfeminine. Perhaps Tennison's closest cousin is Clarice Starling in *The Silence of the Lambs*. But where Starling is young and unseasoned, Tennison is worn and hungry—both fearless and full of uncertainty.

"We see Tennison getting off-kilter, wobbly, as the pressure mounts," says La Plante. "I always pushed the dramatic tension to the absolute limit. I didn't make her an icon. She is very flawed." When La Plante gave the producers the first episode, "They called me in and said, 'We hate her,'" she recalls with a laugh. "They said, 'She is cold. She is not very warm to men. She shows no reaction when they find the body.' And I said, 'You wouldn't expect a doctor to start blubbering at the door, or be shocked or disgusted if he came to see someone dying at your house.'"

La Plante wanted to make *Prime Suspect* as authentic as possible, to provoke controversy, to make people think—and what she saw and wrote about was even harsher than what appears on the screen. Many of the more graphic details of the serial killer's modus operandi were eliminated from the original *Prime Suspect*, which was based on a real case. Also cut was a scene in which Tennison roughly questioned a victim, "which, again, showed her unfeminine side," says La Plante. "But she had to do that to get results, to tease information out of the victim."

In her quest to reflect the complexities of real life, in *Prime Suspect 2* (for which she wrote the scene-by-scene breakdown but not the teleplay), La Plante had wanted a female officer to betray Tennison, not a male one. And La Plante had wanted to see Tennison, the feminist breakthrough, refuse to work under another woman. "I thought that opened up a much more interesting side of her," she explains. "A female competitor after her job— my God, she wasn't going to let her in."

The research for *Prime Suspect 3*, for which La Plante wrote the script, took her into a bleak, hidden world of pedophiles and their young victims. She interviewed vice-squad officers and abused children and spent several days with teenage prostitutes in Cardboard City, a makeshift village under London's Waterloo Bridge. *Prime Suspect 3*, also based on an actual case, was so authentic the pedophile who got away with the crime in real life threatened to sue her. (The attention brought by the show eventually led to his arrest.)

La Plante's walk on the dark side in the service of her characters has taken its toll. She sheds the tears she doesn't allow Tennison, overwhelmed by the horror stories she absorbs and transforms twelve hours a day, seven days a week, chain-smoking at her computer. But she has her own production company now, and she has gone on to write several other acclaimed British series, most recently *The Governor*, about a woman warden at a high-security men's prison. Actress Michelle Pfeiffer has optioned the film rights to *Cold Shoulder*, a La Plante novel about a policewoman in the US. And La Plante has rewritten a draft of the script for the American motion picture version of *Prime Suspect*.

"I think I broke a mold, but I was very lucky to have the mold-breaker so willing to work alongside me," says La Plante. "Now, every detective series has a high-powered woman—unfortunately, usually one too young for the job. I just wish they had more respect for the women who really hold these jobs. They're not twenty-five years old. They are women who have come to that position after many, many years of hard work, moving from squad to squad, working on the streets, dealing with tremendous discrimination all along the way."

THREE NEW PRIME SUSPECTS

by pamela feinsilber

HEN EXECUTIVE PRODUCER Sally Head, creator and scriptwriter Lynda La Plante, series star Helen Mirren, and the rest of the cast began work on the original *Prime Suspect*, no one had any idea of the immense acclaim that would follow. The series won 15 awards in Great Britain and 10 international awards, including two American Emmy Awards for Best Miniseries.

When *Prime Suspect* returned to television, it was in a new form, that of self-contained two-hour movies. The first airs in the US in the fall of 1995. Reflecting *Prime Suspect*'s greater affinity with literature, the dramas will no longer air on *Mystery!* but on public television's premier program, *Masterpiece Theatre*.

PRIME SUSPECT SERIES
Sally Head,
executive producer

THE LOST CHILD
Paul Marcus, producer
John Madden, director
Paul Billing, writer

INNER CIRCLES
Paul Marcus, producer
Sarah Pia Anderson, director
Eric Deacon, writer

THE SCENT OF DARKNESS
Brian Pak, producer
Paul Marcus, director
Guy Hibbert, writer

Robert Glenister's career reflects the British actor's peripatetic life moving among film, television, and theatrical work. He began on the stage: five years with the National Youth Theatre and an appearance with the National Theatre. Then he worked for Thames TV (directed by Mike Newell, whom American audiences know best from his films *Enchanted April* and *An Awfully Big Adventure*). British TV viewers saw him recently in *Persuasion*. And after playing the working-class prime suspect in "The Lost Child," Glenister appeared on London's West End in *The Duchess of Malfi*.

Asked about taking the part of a child sex offender, Glenister says, "The fact that it was in *Prime Suspect* meant I had no hesitation in taking the part."

ROBERT GLENISTER
CHRIS HUGHES

THE LOST CHILD

Tennison, now a detective superintendent but more alone than ever in her private life, leads the search for the abducted child of a young single mother. When a convicted child sex offender emerges as the prime suspect, the clinical psychologist who had treated him points out that the pressure of the investigation could derail him again. Nevertheless, the arrest is badly bungled and turns into a siege, with the suspect's girlfriend and her two daughters held hostage.

Jack Ellis
DET. INSP. TONY MUDDYMAN

LESLEY SHARP, ROBERT GLENISTER, CAROLINE SELBY, CANDICE PAUL

Jack Ellis, who appeared in *Prime Suspect* and *Prime Suspect 2*, has a featured role in "The Lost Child." He says he spent so much time researching the role of Detective Inspector Tony Muddyman that he now feels "like half policeman and half actor. I can spot store detectives a mile off, and this police sense led me to intervene in an attack on a little Indian boy. The great thing about acting is you never have to be anything—you can spend your whole life pretending."

Ellis has also appeared in the British television series *The Knock*, in which he pretended he was an undercover customs and excise investigator. Better yet, he got to play both sides of the criminal fence.

Jane Tennison's continued battles against the job's inherent sexism doesn't mean she welcomes a sister in the squad room. She rides Detective Sergeant Chris Cromwell hard until the latter proves herself by offering a canny inside view of the local class war.

Sophie Stanton came to *Prime Suspect* after appearing in the popular BBC television series *East-Enders*. Her other television credits include *Shine on Harvey Moon* and the BBC's *The Mind Machine*. She has appeared in stage productions as varied as *She Stoops to Conque*r, *The Time of Our Lives*, and *Love's Labour's Lost*. As for motion pictures, Stanton can be seen, with Anthony Hopkins and Debra Winger, in Sir Richard Attenborough's *Shadowlands*.

INNER CIRCLES

When the manager of a country club is found dead in his home, the local police are quick are blame two young people from a rundown housing estate nearby. Once again, Tennison is called to a new station house to head the investigation. This time, the case puts her at odds with both the detective chief inspector she supplanted and the influential voices of the community—particularly the director of the country club (who also heads the police consultative committee) and the dead man's tough, manipulative solicitor—whom Tennison finds a worthy female adversary.

SOPHIE STANTON
DET. SGT. CHRIS CROMWELL

THE SCENT OF DARKNESS

Two women are murdered, and the deaths bear a horrible resemblance to the six for which George Marlow, of the original *Prime Suspect*, is now imprisoned. Is someone imitating him or was the case that gave Tennison her chance a miscarriage of justice? With her objectivity in question, Tennison is suspended from the case. That doesn't stop her from pursuing it, especially when a third woman is abducted and the police have three days in which to find her.

Like Helen Mirren, Stuart Wilson has a foot in both Los Angeles and England, although he gets more work in Hollywood than Mirren does. He's made six feature films there in two years, among them *Lethal Weapon 3* (he played the villain) and Martin Scorsese's *The Age of Innocence*. Most recently, he starred with Sigourney Weaver and Ben Kingsley in Roman Polanski's *Death and the Maiden*, from the play by Ariel Dorfman.

Although he began his career as a film extra in the early sixties, these are the first feature films Wilson has made. He's done theater (he was recently in Chekhov's *Three Sisters* with Vanessa Redgrave) and television, but "film had always eluded me." His most current work was in a British TV drama called *People Versus*.

LOVE AT LAST?

WITH JOYCE REDMAN AS DORIS MARLOW

AS DI HASKONS, RICHARD HAWLEY HASN'T MISSED A *PRIME SUSPECT*

One of the original *Prime Suspect* cast members, Richard Hawley has appeared in every episode—not least of which is "The Scent of Darkness," in which he puts his job on the line for Tennison as he goes outside the department to investigate aspects of the case. Hawley was studying English and sociology at college when he discovered that "acting was for me." He worked steadily with a British company called Impact Theatre. After *Prime Suspect*, he took the lead in a new British drama series, *The Vet*.

"I like it when I'm involved in a program that might change people's thinking somehow—that's why I love being part of *Prime Suspect*," he says. "That was also the appeal of doing *The Vet*."

RICHARD HAWLEY
DET. INSP. RICHARD HASKONS

In her first film: *Age of Consent*

ILDLY SHE MANIFESTED HERSELF, at the age of twenty-three, in a 1969 film called *Age of Consent*. Exotic cocktails called "Sex on the Beach" might have been inspired by her. Wildly she flitted across the screen through the early seventies in *Savage Messiah* and *O Lucky Man!*, from which she went on, in the late seventies and early eighties, to more and stranger wildness (but with classic pretensions) as Caesonia, regal debauchee of Caligula's Rome, and Morgana, half sister of King Arthur. This was wildness on her own terms, almost never suggesting vulnerability: The last time Helen Mirren looked truly vulnerable was in her final scene in the fine 1980 English gangster picture *The Long Good Friday.* As the mistress of crime lord Bob Hoskins, she is being held prisoner in the back of a car, surely on her way to be executed by IRA terrorists, and screaming for help to Hoskins, also on his way to be killed. In the silence of his own death-car, Hoskins cannot hear her and neither can we, and his last glimpse of her is all the more terrifying for how fleeting it is, just as her screaming is all the more terrifying for how soundless it is.

One must see *The Long Good Friday* twice to appreciate Mirren in it, to see how she is the ballast to Hoskins' raging performance. What seems distinctly a one-actor show on first viewing

With the late James Mason in *Age of Consent*

reveals itself as a more precarious balancing act. Interestingly, for many years I misremembered *The Long Good Friday* in a crucial way; my flawed recollection was that Mirren was the traitor in Hoskins' circle, when in fact she was the only one whose loyalty was unimpeachable. This attests, I think, to a cumulative impression of Mirren as hard, and it is a hardness unmitigated by either wildness or beauty. She is pretty in *The Long Good Friday*, if not beautiful; but besides brazenly defying arbitrary criteria of beauty—she is neither overdeveloped nor delicate—her prettiness is not ingratiating. We've never seen the movie star's usual implicit offer of beauty as something to be given away; rather, in Mirren's case it's on loan, for her to use however it suits her purposes. Mirren wouldn't give away her beauty any more than she would give away anything else of her identity, about which she's maintained the sort of integrity that's the luxury of male movie stars. She has conveyed not so much more intelligence than soul as an intelligence that keeps the soul firmly in check, when the soul isn't *useful*; and since on a day-to-day basis the soul is almost never really useful, such an expedient intelligence becomes frightening, particularly in conjunction with a blunt sexuality, and Mirren has always been as bluntly sexual as she is bluntly intelligent.

It's hard to say at what point her film sexuality transformed from the untethered to the consuming, from the consuming to the predatory, from the predatory to the out-and-out depraved. In her most notable movies, Mirren hasn't been merely a femme fatale, a black widow, she's been some modern version of Lilith, the mythic succubus who seduces you in the night and takes your soul with her when she leaves. There's no getting around Mirren's responsibility for this. She chose these parts, after all, and over the last twenty-five years she also created her reputation as a Wild Thing offscreen as well as on, though we will leave it at that.

"Helen Mirren can play anything. She can play a repressed woman, a glamorous woman, a mobster wife. She fully enters the character. She's a psycho-analyst in acting form."

—KIM CHERNIN
AUTHOR, IN MY MOTHER'S HOUSE

In *The Long Good Friday*

> "Doing Caligula
> was like being
> paid well to visit
> a nudist colony."
>
> —HELEN MIRREN
> 1992

Early on, while electrifying audiences on the Shakespearean stage in London, she was as drawn to outré film directors like Michael Powell and Ken Russell and Lindsay Anderson as they were to her. Even accepting the disgraceful circumstances of an industry that offers its best actresses fewer and fewer roles worthy of them, Mirren's choices must speak for themselves, and it's hard to think of another woman who has so routinely, unabashedly, selected projects that explore sex's psychic recesses. In John Boorman's *Excalibur* (1981), she seduced her brother, the king, for the expressed purpose of spawning a monster to succeed him. In Paul Schrader's *The Comfort of Strangers* (1990), she was half of a vampiric Venetian couple wreaking murder and mayhem on a younger couple, for nothing more than the sick pleasure of it. In *Caligula* (1979), she did beastly things with all the other people in *Caligula* doing beastly things, and in *Cal* (1984), she slept with a man half her age who had participated in the murder of her husband. In Peter Greenaway's *The Cook, the Thief, His Wife and Her Lover* (1990), she compelled her husband to eat her dead lover; that he had it coming didn't more easily settle the stomach. Tempted to call Mirren something silly, like the thinking man's sex symbol, more than one man—confronted with Mirren's notions of carnal delight—might find himself thinking, Give me Jennifer Tilly.

But this argument cheats, of course, stacking the deck in favor of Wildness. Not only does it leave out steadier (if more conventional) work in more mainstream (if unremarkable) movies like *The Mosquito Coast* and *2010,* but the above-mentioned *Cal,* for instance, about Irish lives caught up in the Troubles, was hardly what anyone would call kinky. It was probably Mirren's most sympathetic performance; with her hair an unfamiliar auburn, even her prettiness was unfamiliarly soft. And as more time and

more movies have gone by, Mirren has been gradually outdistancing her wild years, and with them her penchant for scandalous movies, in a culture that refuses to recognize a sexual middle ground for its female stars while always cutting male stars slack well into their late fifties or even sixties. Everyone knows Sean Connery and Warren Beatty and Clint Eastwood and Robert

With John Lynch in her award-winning performance in *Cal*

93

With the lads in *Prime Suspect*

Redford (average age: 61) can still be sex symbols, and everyone knows that Sophia Loren and Catherine Deneuve and Julie Christie and Faye Dunaway (average age: 55) cannot. We can bemoan the stupidity and injustice and predictability of this, but that, at least for the moment, doesn't change it. In the years ahead, it will remain to be seen whether the other actresses of Mirren's generation and talent, such as Meryl Streep or Jessica

Lange or Susan Sarandon, or Michelle Pfeiffer or Madeleine Stowe or Jennifer Jason Leigh after them, or Winona Ryder or Uma Thurman or Juliette Lewis after them, can survive what female movie stars have never survived before without becoming either character actors or legends, and that is age. Because while the legends of Bette Davis and Katharine Hepburn and Joan Crawford may have survived, their sexuality, in the eyes of Hollywood and its audience, didn't. Of her peers, or those who deserve to be called her peers, Mirren, at a year shy of fifty, has reached this sexual-cultural Rubicon first. Who would have figured otherwise?

She is there, moreover, without the reservoir of status or exposure that Streep and Lange have stored away for nearly two decades. She was well and confidently into her thirties, after all, when she first began to catch Americans' attention. Like these other actors, she never readily lent herself to being any kind of sex symbol in the first place; and of all of them, Mirren may have been the least willing to suffer, even in her films, either nonsense or victimization. This is most apparent in the vehicle by which she has finally, most memorably, confronted all these issues of age, talent, sexuality, stardom, and male nonsense, a vehicle provided her not by the movies but—big surprise—by British television. The role of Detective Chief Inspector Jane Tennison in *Prime Suspect* is one we can imagine any good American actress killing for, and a few may yet have the opportunity, if rumors that the series will be Americanized as a movie without Mirren prove true. Should any actress actually be so tempted, it would only be a sucker move, of course: Tennison/Mirren looks a lot like one of those Welles/Kane, Bogart/Rick, Karloff/Frankenstein, Pacino/Corleone symbioses another actor has to be a fool to mess with. In the *Prime Suspect* series, Mirren the Hard has apparently

"She's Sarah Bernhardt out of Moll Flanders by Sylvia Plath. Helen Mirren is one of the most complicated, layered actresses working on either side of the Atlantic, and she has a willingness to jump the barriers between high and low culture."

—ELLA TAYLOR
MIRABELLA

"I wanted to do Blue Velvet very much, but I was frightened, and it was so stupid of me. I think you have to dare to go where other people won't as an actor or artist. You have to. That's your function in life, otherwise you may as well be working in a shop."

—HELEN MIRREN

subsumed Mirren the Wild Thing into a characterization at once brittle but ultimately resilient, relentless but sporadically empathetic, constricted but clandestinely sensual; and even as very little wildness appears to leak out of Jane Tennison's self-containment—a pint of bitters with the boys here, a black lover in bed there—she is unavoidably the Wild Card in the masculine world of crime and its grisly investigations and violence, the bitch who won't be pushed around. Yet the triumph seems tainted: She succeeds on male terms, in male fashion. To not be dismissed as a bitch, she has had to become a son of a bitch.

It might be presumptuous and perhaps a bit insulting, considering that Mirren *is* an actor, and a first-rate one, to suggest her incarnation of Tennison is at all autobiographical. But if it's not autobiographical in any factual sense, it is in the metaphoric sense: Both character and actress are at a crucial moment in their lives and careers when they must bring to bear not only everything they have ever known but *everyone they have ever been*. Particularly in a man's world, without the tools of experience and expertise the world offers a man so much more ungrudgingly than it does a woman, Mirren and Tennison must use the tools of their varied personae, as they have been unveiled to themselves and others through the years. The Wild Thing is still somewhere inside Mirren, even as a different sort of wild thing is still inside Tennison; if not a wild and strange sexuality, then a wild and fierce ambition—something, at any rate, the man's world considers wildly unreasonable. Time and again in *Prime Suspect*, Tennison's biggest struggle is to hang onto who she is in the midst of all the machinations and intrigues, keeping both eyes on everything going on around her, all the bastards and bureaucrats trying to undercut her every step, while shooting a quick glance to that dim figure receding into the background, only barely still recognizable as her-

e Cook, the Thief, His Wife and Her Lover

self. It's not a struggle she appears to be winning, which she's smart enough to understand and honest enough to acknowledge as self-betrayal. She's caught between the brute force of her psyche and the soft whisper of her conscience; and the better part of her, which knows she's better than the men she must answer to, might just as soon say the hell with it. But if she did that, not only would the better part never again be able to live with the lesser part, the two might even begin to wonder which is which.

When she was nominated this past year for a supporting actress Academy Award, as "Mrs. King" in *The Madness of King George*, everyone understood it was really for *Prime Suspect*. If *Prime Suspect* had been a motion picture rather than a TV show, an interminable Oscar ceremony could have been abbreviated by suspending nominations altogether and simply shipping the Best Actress statuette off to England. But that would only have deprived us of the chance to see a great actor get her due. It isn't to say that her work in *The Madness of King George* wasn't solid; given a lively script and decent direction, is Mirren ever going to be less? (The performance did win a Best Actress award at this year's Cannes Film Festival.) Another way of looking at it is that *King George* was Mirren's film career come full circle from her first great movie role: As she was to Bob Hoskins in *The Long Good Friday*, she was the ballast to Nigel Hawthorne's raging king, and a second viewing might reveal that what seemed distinctly a one-actor show was a more precarious balancing act all the time. Though when I see the picture again, it isn't likely I will find I've misremembered Helen Mirren in it. I don't misremember anything about her anymore.

"I'm much happier with a good role in a small film than a bad role in a big film."
—HELEN MIRREN
1993

"The Oscars are a soufflé of the moment. People remember your name for a day or two. The dishes still have to be washed."

—HELEN MIRREN
1993

With Nigel Hawthorne in
The Madness of King George

PORT OF STRANGERS　　　CALIGULA

PASCALI'S ISLAND

Excalibur © Orion Picture Company; *The Mosquito Coast* © The Saul Zaentz Company

filmography
By Pamela Feinsilber

Age of Consent (1969)
One of the last films directed by famed British writer-producer-director Michael Powell, Mirren's first movie stars James Mason as an artist who escapes to Australia's Great Barrier Reef, where he finds inspiration in the feisty young girl whom he persuades to pose for him—Mirren, of course.

Savage Messiah (1972)
The young savage is sculptor Henri Gaudier-Brzeska (played by Scott Antony), who died in WW I at age 24. Directed with his usual intensity by Ken Russell, the movie chronicles the young man's platonic affair with Sophie Brzeska (Dorothy Tutin); Mirren has third billing as a suffragette.

O Lucky Man! (1973)
Continuing her streak of working with top British film directors, Mirren plays rich, rebellious Patricia in Lindsay Anderson's picaresque allegory of a coffee salesman who pushes his way to the top, falls, and rises again. Her costars include Malcolm McDowell, Ralph Richardson, and Rachel Roberts. *

Caligula (1979)
Called "filmdom's first $15 million porno movie" (reviewer Leonard Maltin), *Caligula* has sex and violence sufficient to bring

101

it an X rating, though there's a far tamer R-rated version around, too. Mirren says frankly she played the voracious Caesonia for the money, and at least she got to work with Malcolm McDowell, Peter O'Toole, and John Gielgud—not to mention buying that 100 acres of wooded land in Scotland. *

The Long Good Friday (1980)
No sex but plenty of violence in this well-received film about a crime boss whose world collapses over an Easter weekend in contemporary London. Mirren plays the sophisticated companion of underworld entrepreneur Bob Hoskins. *

Hussy (1980)
This melodrama about a hooker, her boyfriend, illicit drugs, and a bunch of gangsters never makes it onto Mirren's résumé. *

The Fiendish Plot of Dr. Fu Manchu (1980)
Even Mirren didn't remember she played a London policewoman in Peter Sellers' last picture. The film was considered painfully unfunny. Enough said. *

Excalibur (1981)
A sexually aware telling of the legend of King Arthur, directed by John Boorman and starring Nicol Williamson and Nigel Terry; Mirren is an appropriately seductive (as in seducing her half brother, the king) Morgana. *

Priest of Love (1981)
Mirren has a small role in this big-name-cast depiction of the last years of author D.H. Lawrence, which stars Ian McKellen, Janet Suzman, John Gielgud, Ava Gardner, and Sarah Miles. *

A Midsummer Night's Dream (1982)

Finally, a starring role—and a regal part no less, as Hermia—in Peter Hall's film version of Shakespeare's frothy fantasy, in which the king (Peter McEnery) and queen of a fairy kingdom draw humans into their amorous battles. *

Cal (1984)

Mirren won a Best Actress award at Cannes for her portrayal of Marcella, the widow of a murdered Protestant policeman in Northern Ireland with whom young John Lynch falls in love, despite his IRA involvement in her husband's death. *

2010 (1984)

Mirren draws on her paternal heritage to play Russian cosmonaut Tanya Kirbuk in this follow-up to *2001*, directed by Peter Hyams from Arthur C. Clarke's novel *The Sentinel*. A joint US-Soviet crew sets out to discover what went wrong on the original Discovery spaceflight. Costars include Roy Scheider, John Lithgow, Bob Balaban, and Keir Dullea. *

White Nights (1985)

Here she plays a Russian ballerina—now head of the Bolshoi Ballet—who crosses paths with Mikhail Baryshnikov (as a Soviet ballet star who defected, then finds himself back in the USSR after a forced plane landing) and Gregory Hines (as the American expatriate who's supposed to encourage him not to leave again). The film was directed by Taylor Hackford. *

The Mosquito Coast (1986)

Harrison Ford is a monomaniacal inventor who moves his family—including Mirren as stalwart, long-suffering "Mother" and

River Phoenix as his son—to a remote village in Honduras, there to build his version of Utopia. Paul Schrader wrote the screenplay from Paul Theroux's novel; Peter Weir directed. *

Pascali's Island (1988)
Ben Kingsley is an underused Turkish spy who joins forces with a mysterious Brit, Charles Dance, not knowing he wants to steal an archeological treasure from a Greek island under Turkish rule. Mirren plays a Viennese artist who falls in love with Dance after a nude Mediterranean swim. *

When the Whales Came (1989)
Mirren's costars in this conservationist fable, set on a remote British island during WW I, are Paul Scofield, two children, and a group of narwhal whales. *

The Cook, the Thief, His Wife and Her Lover (1990)
Debauchery in an opulent setting: Mirren is the wife, bullied by her beyond-vulgar ganglord husband, who frolics with her bookish lover in the cook's posh restaurant. Her lingerie and her revenge were critics' focal points. Peter Greenaway wrote and directed; Michael Gambon costars. *

The Comfort of Strangers (1990)
Creepy spouses Mirren and Christopher Walken are the spiders who lure Rupert Everett and Natasha Richardson into their web of sadomasochistic games in an ornate Venice apartment. Harold Pinter wrote the screenplay from a novel by Ian McEwan; Paul Schrader directed. *

Where Angels Fear to Tread (1991)

In this adaptation of E.M. Forster's first novel, Mirren embarks for Tuscany after the death of her husband. To the chagrin of her in-laws, she marries a much younger man; then she dies in childbirth. Italy has a chance to charm the stuffy Brits (Helena Bonham-Carter, Judy Davis, Rupert Graves) when the family sets out to "rescue" her son. *

The Hawk (1993)

The flip side of *Prime Suspect*: Mirren plays Annie Marsh, an ordinary suburban housewife married to an ordinary man whom she begins to suspect may be a vicious (he gouges out the eyes of his victims) serial killer.

The Madness of King George (1994)

The relatively small part of Charlotte, King George III's German-born queen, brought Mirren her second Cannes Best Actress award and an Academy Award nomination. (Her costar, Nigel Hawthorne, was also nominated.) Alan Bennett's screenplay, based on his 1991 play, looks at court intrigues surrounding the bizarre syndrome that first afflicted King George in 1788. The other stars are Rupert Everett, Ian Holm, Rupert Graves, and Amanda Donohoe. *

* *Available on video cassette*

With John Hurt in *A Month in the Country*, London, 1994

life in the theater

By Benedict Nightingale

HERE CAN BE FEW MORE TAXING roles for an actress, especially a British actress, than Natalya Petrovna in Turgenev's *A Month in the Country*. She's the helpless victim of the passion—deeply embarrassing to someone who is the middle-aged wife of an important landowner—she comes to feel for her son's handsome tutor. She's also a jealous monster, selfish and treacherous enough to lure her ward into confessing her own love for the young man and then, to undermine their relationship, marry the girl off to a foolish old admirer. Even by the standards of Russian drama, the range and volatility of emotions this predicament produces is extraordinary.

Natalya refuses to acknowledge her feelings, joyfully embraces them, renounces them in self-disgust, argues with them, and tries to fulfill them; she must sometimes do this, and more, within the span of a few sentences. And there's even more to the character: fear of aging, self-mockery, vindictiveness, grief, and a girlishness that can be simultaneously sweet and off-putting, as if Lady Capulet were passing herself off as Juliet or Cleopatra as Ophelia.

This was the challenge facing Helen Mirren when she played

"You have to have a magic actress play Natalya Petrovna—somebody who has consummate theater skills, vocally and physically, and a leading actor's personality."

—BILL BRYDEN
DIRECTOR, A MONTH IN
THE COUNTRY, LONDON

Natalya Petrovna in London in April 1994, and to say that she overcame it is to understate the case. Critics should be as cautious of using the word "triumph" as of the word "masterpiece," but for once the term was deserved. It was not only the completeness of the performance that was impressive; not only the blend of intelligence and emotional power that was remarkable; not only that all her feelings, whether from the heart or the stomach or the less mentionable glands beneath, seemed at times to be at work all at once. It was that Ms. Mirren engineered some of the trickiest transitions world drama has to offer, with an adroitness I don't think any other actress could match.

I felt I was seeing an actress in her prime giving the great performance that, despite ups and downs, she had long promised. Nor was I alone in that judgment. "Simply amazing," declared the *Observer*. "Acting of the highest calibre, technically brilliant, infectiously funny, and shot through with real depth of feeling," added the *Daily Telegraph*. The Sunday *Express* was moved to recall Dorothy Parker's celebrated put-down of Katharine Hepburn's Cleopatra, running the gamut of emotions from A to B. "There are not enough letters in the alphabet to describe the emotions explored by Helen Mirren," its critic wrote.

Though the performance seemed fluent and effortless, it was surely not easily won. I've seen Helen Mirren on various stages for a quarter of a century now, and, without either of us realizing it, I've been watching her prepare for just such a climax. On the one hand, her work has always had an emotional force and a sensuality rare in British actresses, who are regularly accused of performing from the neck up and ignoring the parts below. On the other hand, she has displayed an equally remarkable delight in taking interpretive and technical risks.

Actually, my first experiences of Ms. Mirren's work left me

slightly disappointed, for I had heard about this precocious young woman who had brought a most un-English oomph to the female lead in a production of *Antony and Cleopatra* staged by Britain's National Youth Theatre. But her Hero, in *Much Ado About Nothing*—admittedly one of the Bard's most characterless ingenues—seemed to add little to the Royal Shakespeare Company's 1968 season, and her playing of Cressida, in *Troilus and Cressida*, even less. She played that seductive and treacherous female as a Trojan teenybopper, a flirt and a tease who actually fell on her back and satirically opened her legs when the subject of sex came up. That struck me as an excessively obvious and superficial way of suggesting the character's fickleness, but the real trouble was that Ms. Mirren seemed to be forcing the physicality. "Her wanton spirits look out at every joint and motive of her body," says Ulysses, who speaks in as near to Shakespeare's voice as anybody in the play. And indeed they did, but in a self-conscious, deliberate, even awkward way.

But as I should have realized, this was not a performer content to accept her own limitations and the orthodox expectations of others. Rather, here was a young actress who refused to be intimidated by the traditions of Stratford and was prepared to try difficult, dangerous things, even if the result wasn't conventionally successful. And her next years with the RSC were ones of growth for Ms. Mirren. She played Julia in Robin Phillips' larky revival of Shakespeare's *Two Gentlemen of Verona*, which was set on and around the beach in modern Rimini; an oppressed Ophelia who showed her repressed fury at the callous male world in *Hamlet* by going mad; and a vigorous, passionate Lady Anne in *Richard III*. This last is a particularly tough part, since the character, the widow of Edward, Prince of Wales, must enter behind the corpse of his father, Henry VI, and within minutes allow herself

From her Broadway debut, 1995

to be wooed and won by their murderer, Richard himself. Ms. Mirren started by whacking Norman Rodway, who played this part, on the back with the huge cross her retinue was carrying, as if to exorcise him, and ended by giggling and dabbling lips with him only yards from the king's bleeding body. Saint Joan was, so to speak, transformed into Jezebel—on the face of it an absurdity, but an absurdity in keeping with Terry Hands' deliberately grotesque production, and, once again, boldly done.

Her finest performance during this period was as the title character in Strindberg's *Miss Julie*, again for Robin Phillips and the RSC, in 1971. She brought what was becoming her trademark full-bloodedness to the role, raging and roaring in upper-class contempt at Jean, the valet who had seduced her; but it was the character's psychosexuality that mainly preoccupied her. Her hands quivered, kneaded her handkerchief, flailed frantically, blindly, at her wooer, as if her body was in a state of civil war, in terror and disgust driving her away from him and then, with a sort of morbid, self-destructive fascination, to him, into his arms and his power. Nor was that all, for Ms. Mirren found moments of tenderness in the role, as well as a touching pathos. I can still hear her saying, "What is love? Do you know what love is?" as if distantly sensing the existence of emotions she was doomed never to feel.

Perhaps her portrayal remained a little planned and lacking in fluency; the rivets joining her ideas together still sometimes showed; but this time it could be attributed to the emotional jumps and bumps the "naturalist" Strindberg had deliberately injected into his dialogue. By now, few critics could be unaware that here was a major actress in the making. She thought originally, she expressed feeling physically, and, increasingly, she was integrating thought and feeling into a coherent whole. Thanks to the

As *Miss Julie* with the Royal
Shakespeare Company, 1971

RSC's voice department, she also knew how to make verse meaningful and natural without destroying its rhythms. All this, plus her interest in female psychosexuality, Ms. Mirren now brought to one of the great classical roles. I saw her Lady Macbeth twice, in Stratford in 1974 and a year later in London. I recall feeling that her performance had grown in the interim—but I didn't realize how important her interpretation actually was.

To perhaps overgeneralize about Lady Macbeths: In eighteenth-century portrayals, she tended to be a powerful and terrible woman, forcing a loving but weak Macbeth into regicide. Late in the nineteenth century, a more sentimentally conceived, "womanly" Lady Macbeth appeared, one whom a cowardly Macbeth manipulated into giving him permission to commit murder, and who was a caring enough wife to take the blame herself. It is only relatively recently that the sexual relationship of the Macbeths began to be explored, at least on the British stage. The American academic Marvin Rosenberg, whose brilliant book *Masks of Macbeth* chronicles the play's performance history, has some examples of French actresses attempting to portray what he calls "the sensual Lady"; but according to his testimony, Helen Mirren pioneered what's now become a common, almost customary interpretation of the role.

When she hugged Nicol Williamson's Macbeth, returning with news of the witches' prophecy, both her seductiveness and her scorn made it clear that her favors depended on a rather extreme display of "manliness" by him. As one critic put it, her body was the reward for an obediently performed murder. And her jubilant cry of "My husband!" after he had killed Duncan reemphasized that, though the tragedy might end on the battlefield, it had begun in bed. While a sensual bond might be enough to create murderers, however, it is not enough to sustain them—

With Nicol Williamson in *Macbeth,* Royal Shakespeare Company, 1974

or so Trevor Nunn's production proceeded to show.

Using a white napkin, Ms. Mirren's Lady Macbeth tried and failed to wipe the blood her husband's daggers had left on her hands. She also was badly shaken by a second look at Duncan's body, which Nunn actually brought onstage. And gradually she went to pieces, developing the nervous tic, a compulsive washing of those once-bloody hands, that she was to repeat to great effect in the sleepwalking scene. But a key reason for her decline was rejection by the husband she herself had implicitly threatened to reject sexually. He roughly and rudely sent her packing when he was contemplating Banquo's murder, kept her ignorant of its execution, and left her helplessly watching ("Why do you keep alone, of sorriest fancies your companions making?") his increasing isolation and paranoia. Instead of his depending on her, she found she depended on him, and was destroyed by that dependence.

This reading does not distort Shakespeare's original, but it does give the play a contemporary twist and, as a consequence, has been enormously influential. Few actors and actresses now feel they can ignore what might be called the sexual politics of the Macbeths' dark and sinister marriage. That was largely Mirren's achievement—and what did she do next? Launch instantly into two difficult and demanding roles, one in Chekhov's *The Seagull*, the other the leading role in *Teeth 'n' Smiles*, a new play by a rising young dramatist named David Hare.

On the face of it, the characters she played could not have been more different. Chekhov's Nina usually comes across as an innocent bloom, a guileless girl who naively wants to become an actress and is deflowered and destroyed by Trigorin, the famous writer she foolishly hero-worships. By comparison, Maggie in *Teeth 'n' Smiles* might be Snow White on the skids. She is a 1960s figure at sea in the 1970s, a singer who has hit the bottle and the hard drugs in despair over years of making purposeless music and having loveless sex. But as Ms. Mirren played them, the two women didn't come from separate species. Both were sentient women, and conceived in the tough-minded, unsentimental way that was becoming another of her trademarks.

Her Maggie sneered, snarled, pouted, and sobbed her way through an evening spent with her backup group at a gig at a Cambridge college ball, and ended up drunk and angry enough to set fire to the tent in which they were performing. During that time, she talked a great deal about pain, need, and the other emotions that had once inspired her singing, but it was a nice question as to whether she still knew what any of it meant. It was a troubling picture of someone who had lost her capacity to care, perhaps even to feel, and who seemed increasingly out of touch with the reality she made such a show of hating.

Her Nina was, if anything, more shocking. The character had become knowing, vulgar, a literary groupie in the making, as much in love with celebrity as any Hollywood hanger-on. Indeed, she injected a sort of erotic greed into the word that obsessed her, "fame," and seemed thrilled, not troubled, at the hint that she might one day star in a Trigorin short story about the killing of a symbolic seagull. And Ms. Mirren didn't leave the portrait there. When her Nina reappeared in Act Four, she gave the impression not of a badly wilted flower but of a plant that had grown hardier with time. Mirren found dignity, endurance, a strength in adversity where other actresses had seen little but smashed dreams and spiritual emptiness.

It was an original performance, but, as with her Lady Macbeth, well justified by the text. Then came an equally unpredictable assortment of roles: Queen Margaret in Shakespeare's

"I've been an actress for quite a long time. You have moments of recognition and moments when you're struggling, and you know both will pass. The important thing is to keep going, if you can."

—HELEN MIRREN
1993

Henry VI in 1977, as much a study in deviant psychosexuality let loose as in the love of power; Isabella in *Measure for Measure* in 1979, a portrait of a woman painfully freed from her own emotional rigidity; and the title role in Webster's *The Duchess of Malfi* in 1980, a wonderful portrait of strong feeling and straight dealing, courage, integrity, and pride. Her rendering of the Duchess' cry after she has lost husband and children and is about to lose her own life, "I am the Duchess of Malfi still," rang through the theater with a magnificent defiance.

And so, in 1981, to Brian Friel's *The Faith Healer*, in which she brought a blend of tenderness, love, yearning, frustration, and pain to the role of the widow of an itinerant medicine man. And, in 1983, to the lead part in Middleton and Dekker's seldom-performed Jacobean comedy, *The Roaring Girl.* The title character, Moll Cutpurse, was based on a real woman of the period, and in the play she wears breeches, smokes a pipe, and confounds the men around her with her pluck and guile. It is a lively role—T.S. Eliot called her "a real, perpetually real, and human figure"—and Ms. Mirren played it with swaggering bravado. You could not exactly say she gave the play a feminist twist because it already had one, thanks to its authors' delight in a heroine who does traditionally "male" things with energy and self-belief. But her work emphasized that, if directors sought an actress capable of robustly extending conventional notions of what a woman is, Helen Mirren should be at the forefront of their thinking.

To that extent she is, I suppose, a feminist actress. But the description makes me uneasy because it suggests she has a quasi-political agenda to pursue. That was not apparent when she played the protagonist in William Mastrosimone's *Extremities* in 1984, even though the text invited it. She had to capture a would-be rapist, tie him up, and decide whether or not to kill him, yet

With Mike Gwilym in *The Duchess of Malfi*, Royal Exchange, Manchester, 1980

Ms. Mirren did more than express outrage and retaliatory fury. That, you felt, would have been too easy a choice for her. She went on to present us with a woman whose veneer of civilization, perhaps even whose sanity, came close to cracking under the pressure of anger. By the end, her feelings included a kind of exhausted compassion for the man she was tormenting and a certain horror at what, she now recognized, was her own capacity for sadism. It was less a case of good versus evil—as it had been when Farrah Fawcett played the role in New York—than of good contaminated by evil.

This was a daring interpretation, especially at the dawning of the age of political correctness, but it did emphasize what Helen Mirren was and is all about. She isn't interested in fashion or show. She isn't interested in playing likable, sympathetic characters. What seems to attract her is the chance to explore exciting roles as fully as she can and, in doing so, imaginatively to expose every aspect of herself, dark or light or in between. What attracts her is human completeness. The only trouble is that, as she moves through her middle age, the opportunities become fewer, as they do for any serious actress and certainly for any classical actress. Glenda Jackson, who has since become a member of Parliament, once said that she didn't see the point of remaining in the theater in order to play the Nurse in *Romeo and Juliet.* Ms. Mirren, I suspect, would echo that sentiment.

At any rate, she appears seldom on the stage these days. A fine pair of performances in Arthur Miller's double bill, *Two-Way Mirror*, in 1989, was followed in 1991 by a rare error of judgment, the role of a larky prostitute in a bad farce called *Sex Please, We're Italian*; and then came redemption and success in *A Month in the Country*. What's next is anyone's guess. There are roles—Ranyevskaya in *The Cherry Orchard*, Arkadina in *The Seagull*—

With Kevin McNally in *Extremities*,
Duchess Theatre, 1984

worth Ms. Mirren's attention. Another go at Cleopatra would be welcome; the last time she tackled the role, back in 1983, she emphasized the character's mischievous, spirited, affectionate aspects and did not find great texture or depth in her passion.

It would also be nice if a contemporary playwright would rise to the challenge of writing a role large and intense enough for her very special talents. The British theater is not so rich it can afford to lose an actress with her qualities of mind and heart and, as Natalya Petrovna showed, her ability to fuse the two.

"I wanted to be a
female Alec
Guinness. I wanted
to be able to take
on amazing subtle
personalities and
completely change
my physical
appearance by the
flicker of a fin-
ger and the twitch
of an eye—just to
be different."

—HELEN MIRREN
1971

With Michael Gambon in *Antony
and Cleopatra*, Royal Shakespeare
Company, 1982

121

California days; with Carinthia West after winning
the Cannes Best Actress award, 1985

from a friend

By Carinthia West

A WELL-KNOWN PERSON WRITING his autobiography recently placed an advertisement in the classified section of the London *Times*. It read, "If you can remember where I was between 1969 and 1979, please let me know." I feel somewhat the same when it comes to dating the time and place Helen Mirren and I met. A friendship contains so many shared memories (and some that the other person *doesn't* remember), intertwined experiences, ups, downs, and, sometimes, long periods of separation. The older one gets, the more sorting out one's friendships becomes like taking treasured jewelry out of a strongbox. You may not wear these pieces much, but each item represents a different part of your life, each gem has its own sparkle. And so it is with Helen, whose generosity, vision, courageousness, and grace count as much, if not more, to me than her extraordinary talent and fame.

When did she first come into my life? One summer, I believe, sometime in the early seventies. My family comes from Stratford-on-Avon, and one day an old friend, Prince George Galitzine, came over with his new girlfriend. I suppose I must have vaguely known of the actress Helen Mirren (mainly because of her tabloid title, "Sex Queen of the RSC"), just as I had vaguely heard that

Helen Mirren, circa 1970

George was living in a sort of "aristocratic commune" nearby. This was a farm called "Parsenn Sally," run by a formidably amusing relative of George's called Lady Sarah Ponsonby and at which, it was rumored, Princess Margaret stayed from time to time. Helen and George lived there, along with a laid-back array of artists, musicians, and other well-connected itinerants. Helen commuted daily to the Royal Shakespeare Theatre at Stratford, playing a variety of roles (brilliantly, of course) and returning each night to bongo drums and fiveskin spliffs. Pretty cool, I thought, when I first met her, spilling out of George's mini with high red lace-up boots and a big smile. I think they brought a huge dog with them.

We met not long after she had come back from a year's tour of Africa with Royal Shakespeare Company director Peter Brook, taking mime, music, and theater to the bush tribes. An actress thinking only of her career might have refused to go; not Helen. On her left hand she still bears a momento, the tattooed mark of two interlocking crosses, which means "equal and opposite," a symbol that suits her down to the ground.

I remember feeling an instant affinity to this down-to-earth girl without any actressy airs or graces. It was the beginning of a friendship that has sustained through countless changes of boyfriends, countries, crises, and all the wears and tears of living. As a writer, I have perhaps a slightly voyeuristic relationship with my close friends, and as a former actress, I feel it with Helen and other actress friends most of all. Their talent and muscle in the acting world represents a side of me unused (and frankly, I'd rather watch them up on that stage or screen than be there myself). They do for me what I, perhaps, do for them, which is to act out the unconscious parts of ourselves that life, with its strict need to focus, does not give us time to reach or express. I recall

Helen telling me once, in Los Angeles, "I wish I could write," and when I said, "Yes, but of course you can, it's just another extension of your talent," she shyly confided that she had started to write a novel but didn't think it was good enough. She said she didn't have the application, the discipline, to sit alone in a room, without a director telling her what to do. I wonder if she ever finished it. The lead character's name was Manchester. I remember thinking that was a great start.

Over the years, I had loads of opportunities to be startled again by Helen's sheer talent, and to see up close how a few roles reflected the state her offstage life was in at the time. While she was appearing in David Hare's play *Teeth 'n' Smiles*, in which she played a self-destructive, Janis Joplin-type character, she began to party wildly—in part maybe because, as she confessed to me, she was so scared of singing onstage, and because to find the character of Maggie she had to plumb the "nasty depths" of herself. She changed boyfriends soon after. James Wedge is a respected British photographer with whom I often worked as a model, dark, quietly funny, and hugely talented. He and Helen made an attractive pair as well as a highly creative team; she would often style his photo shoots. But a lot of their time was spent at their country cottage, where they liked nothing better than to don their oldest clothes and muck around in the vegetable patch. Helen has always loved gardening. Years later, she told me for a magazine article that her idea of happiness was to spread manure on her roses: "It may look and sound like bullshit, but whatever makes my roses happy, makes me happy."

A far cry from the usual self-indulgent actress quote, and reflective of her personal philosophy of serenity; but then, the great thing about Helen is that she has never been self-absorbed, has always been curious about life, people, and what makes them

With costume designer Theadora
van Runkle in a Paris café

tick. This genuine interest is what makes her acting superior to so many others. Her curiosity has led her to take some strange excursions, too, such as her role in the Bob Guccione romp *Caligula* (which she unashamedly did for the money—it bought her a plot of land in Scotland and a new Honda, as I remember). She tells the funniest story about accepting that job. Guccione had taken her and the film's director, Tinto Brass, to dinner, where he told her, "I've got Malcolm McDowell, the *best* film actor. I've got Sir John Gielgud, the *best* stage actor. I've got Peter O'Toole, the *best* movie star. I've got Gore Vidal, the *best* screenplay writer." Brass leaned over and whispered to her, "To make the *worst* movie." Later she would breathe incredulously on the phone from Rome, where they were shooting the picture, "God, Carinth, you should see the orgy scenes!"

Her own sensuality was never in question, and invariably, every few years a new boyfriend would come along. (She's been able to remain the best of friends with all of them.) James Wedge was followed by Liam Neeson, then an unknown actor whom she met while making *Excalibur.* I can see them walking together down the streets of his hometown of Ballymena in Northern Ireland: Helen petite in her trademark pair of high lace-up boots (she has always loved stilettos, but anything red or with laces was total Helen), Liam the gentle giant at her side, as the lace curtains of the small town twitched and the local ladies twittered, "Aye, Liam, he's brought home that actress, that Helen Mirren." She charmed them, of course, as she charmed all "ordinary, everyday" people. In London, they lived in a house that Helen had owned for several years, in Doria Road, Fulham. That was originally a working-class section that soon became trendy and upwardly mobile. I can remember sitting with Helen in her drawing-room, all stripped pine and white lace, listening to car doors slam and

With actor John Hurt, actress Amanda Donohoe (middle), and actress Miranda Richardson

129

With actress Eileen Atkins and
actor Jason Robards

nasal upper-class British accents—"Hello, dahling, I'm home, anyone seen my tennis racquet?"—and Helen grimacing and saying in that beautifully modulated voice, "I think it's time to move."

And so she did, but this time over the water to Los Angeles, leaving Liam to pursue his own acting career (and we know about that now). She rented an apartment in the same block Bette Davis lived on, and one day she rang up in a state of great excitement. "Bette Davis wants to meet *me*!" For some time after, she would take tea with the aging star. She was working on a big science-fiction picture, and she loved driving through the gates of the studio in her rented red convertible Mustang, feeling that she'd finally arrived in Hollywood after those teenage years frequenting her local cinema in Southend. But the down side would hit her as soon as a film was finished, and she would confess to that old insecurity: "Will I ever work again?" She would, of course, but first she must trail 'round the inevitable casting agents like anyone else, braving their plastic-smiled assistants ("What did you say your name was again?") and responding politely to lines like "I loved that film you did, you know, *The Long Goodbye*." They meant *The Long Good Friday*, of course, but she took it all with great good humor.

By this time, we were sharing a funky stuccoed flat on Orange Drive, off La Brea. I was impressed that Helen insisted on taking the "maid's room," the smallest room at the back of the flat, because, she said, it made her feel more at home. We shared the flat with a willowy blonde photographer named Rory Flynn, daughter of Errol, and from that experience Helen and I came up with a sitcom idea we named *English Muffins*, about two English girls and an American, in its outrageousness a sort of forerunner to *Absolutely Fabulous*. Neither of us could believe it when we

"I had this romantic dream of starting again, from scratch, living in a seedy hotel on Sunset Boulevard. Instead, I live in a big house with a swimming pool."

—HELEN MIRREN
1993

With her partner, director Taylor
Hackford, at the 1995 Academy Awards

sold the treatment to Universal for $3,000. Visions of a long-running hit made us break out the champagne, but it was not to be. Tracy Ullman had developed something similar, and our project was shelved. With her customary generosity, and knowing I was as broke as a skunk, Helen made me keep all the money. I bought a secondhand Buick and blessed her every day.

She was out when I took a phone call from the producers of *Cal*, and I was able to give her the message that she'd won the Cannes Best Actress award. That's when another bottle of champagne came out. A few weeks later, she went off to shoot *White Nights*, a film directed by Taylor Hackford, very hot in Hollywood after the success of his *An Officer and a Gentleman*. I seem to remember she wasn't all that keen on him in the beginning, a fact I tease her with now. Taylor seemed the man to finally win her heart, which, despite her numerous men friends, I had always felt she had been fully in control of. Now she was in love, passionately, fully, and sometimes jealously (although never with her close friends). It was a joy to see her, actually, although she occasionally returned to our flat and the maid's room swearing never to speak to that man again. Rory and I always foiled the "I'm out if he calls" routine (we both secretly thought he was great for her) and would disloyally purr, "Taylor, yes, she's right here. Just hang on a sec." I'm so glad we were such traitorous friends as I watch them pottering around their sprawling Hollywood hills garden more than ten years later, discussing the various merits of tropical plants. I think his pure outdoors no-bullshit American masculinity constantly fascinates and challenges her, and her European elegance, grace, and femininity totally absorb and intrigue him. There's much more to it than that, but it would be rude of me to comment further!

As I write this in London on July 26, I realize it's Helen's

"She was always the girl who asked for more, always acting as though living life to anything less than the hilt was an affront to life itself. An essence of Sixties London lives uncompromised within her, no matter where she may be making her home."

—ALAN FRANK
LONDON TIMES

133

birthday, so in a couple of hours I will call her and wish her a very happy one. I can't remember which it is, but it doesn't matter because Helen is one of those rare women who are essentially ageless, in the manner of French actresses like Jeanne Moreau or Simone Signoret, though such women are practically unheard of in Hollywood. Of course, now that *Prime Suspect* has been such a huge hit, she no longer has to face the inane responses of uninitiated agents. Everyone knows who she is. As Jane Tennison, that no-nonsense, straight-talking detective chief inspector with the curiously feminine insecure side, Helen has finally found a part in contemporary life that she can breathe, walk, and embody. Who would have guessed at its success? "I'm playing this police-woman," she told me one day from Manchester, "it's quite tough, actually, but it gives me a chance to act with a lot of great blokes and eat in Indian restaurants."

Perhaps Manchester brought her luck (remember her novel?), but at last she no longer has to fear the parts drying up or, perhaps, worry about that dreaded gap that all actresses over forty fear. With Jane Tennison, she has opened a window to a whole new "infinite variety" in her later years, and we who are lucky enough to be among her friends can only stand back and say we never had any doubts. Happy birthday, Helen, you're the best friend anyone could wish for.

"What would I like on my gravestone? How about: Feel free to sit down. No, I've got it: Dance here."

—HELEN MIRREN

contributors

Steve Erickson is a Los Angeles-based writer and novelist. He has written about film for *Elle, Esquire,* and *Rolling Stone* and is a former film critic for the *LA Weekly.* He has written about cultural and political subjects for *The New York Times, Details,* and *Los Angeles Times Magazine.* His novels include *Arc D'X, Tours of the Black Clock, Rubicon Beach, Days Between Stations,* and the forthcoming *Amnesiascope.* He also wrote a political memoir, *Leap Year.*

Pamela Feinsilber, whose background is in literature and the arts, has lived in several countries, including Malta, Japan, and Switzerland. She has written and edited for a number of publications, among them *Ms., Mother Jones, Cosmopolitan, Saturday Review, San Francisco Focus, Tokyo Journal, 'Teen, California Lawyer, San Francisco Chronicle, In These Times, The People's Almanac,* and *The Book of Lists.*

Louise Kollenbaum's work is inspired by art, politics, and nature. She has been founding art director of *Mother Jones* magazine, design director of Banana Republic, and creative director of Smith & Hawken. She collaborated as creative director with *Doonesbury*'s Garry Trudeau in product development. She is currently developing products, packaging books, and contributing to a variety of magazines.

Benedict Nightingale is chief drama critic of the *Times* of London. He has been writing about the theater since 1964 for a number of British publications, including the *Manchester Guardian, New Statesman, Sunday Times, Daily Telegraph, Observer, Independent,* and *Standard.* He also contributes regularly to *The New York Times* and other publications. He has taught theater and English at the University of Michigan and is the author of two books, *A Reader's Guide to Fifty Modern British Plays* and *Fifth Row Center: A Critic's Year On and Off Broadway.*

Amy Rennert is editor-in-chief of *San Francisco Focus* magazine, which under her leadership has garnered dozens of national and regional awards. She has written major profiles of leading arts, media, sports, and political figures, among them Bill Moyers, Martina Navratilova, Terry McMillan, and Gloria Steinem. Her interviews with novelists Pat Conroy and Armistead Maupin won the 1992 and 1993 Best Interview awards from the Western Publishers Association. She has also written for *Playboy* magazine and the *Los Angeles Times* syndicate.

Tom Shales is the Pulitzer Prize-winning television editor and chief television critic of the *Washington Post*. His column has been syndicated since 1979 to more than 120 newspapers. He has won the American Society of Newspaper Editors writing award and was named Best Critic Writing for a Newspaper by the *Washington Journalism Review*. He lives in Arlington, Virginia, with three television sets.

Marilee Strong is senior writer for *San Francisco Focus* magazine. She is the recipient of numerous journalism honors, including a National Headliner award, four "Maggies," and a William Allen White award for her magazine writing. Her work has also been featured in the *Atlanta Constitution*, *New York Daily News*, *San Diego Union*, and on National Public Radio. She is a graduate of the Columbia University Graduate School of Journalism, where her work earned her a Pulitzer Fellowship to cover the war in Mozambique.

Amy Taubin writes on film for *The Village Voice*. A contributing editor to *Sight and Sound* magazine, she is also writing a book on independent films, to be published by Doubleday.

Carinthia West was a model and an actress before deciding that a writing career gave her both freedom and stimulation without the insecurity. She has written profiles for *Cosmopolitan*, *Redbook*, *US*, and other magazines, and she was style editor of the *LA Weekly* before returning to England. A contributing editor for Britain's *Marie Claire*, she is currently working on a book about transformational times in women's lives.

James Wolcott quit college in the early seventies to work for *The Village Voice*, where he was the television critic for seven years. He has had regular columns on books and pop culture in *Harper's* and *Esquire* and has frequently contributed to the *New Republic* and the *London Observer*. For nine years, he was a contributing editor at *Vanity Fair*, where he profiled Sean Penn and Camille Paglia, among others. He is currently a staff writer at *The New Yorker* and is working on his first novel.

permissions

We thank the following writers for their contributions:
Tom Shales reviews: "Prime Suspect": ©1992, *Washington Post* Writers Group. Reprinted with permission. "Prime Suspect 3": © 1994, *Washington Post* Writers Group. Reprinted with permission. Amy Taubin review: "Prime Suspect 2": Reprinted by permission of the author and *The Village Voice*.

Special thanks to Ellen Frey and the staff at Michael Shepley Public Relations.

Thanks also to Karen Johnson and the staff at WGBH.

We would like to acknowledge Mobil Corporation, which has underwritten *Mystery!* and *Masterpiece Theatre* since their inception.

Prime Suspect photographs supplied courtesy of Granada Television Limited. The *Prime Suspect* title is owned by Granada Television and is used with its express permission.

We acknowledge the following photographers and agencies for their contributions:
©Mark Hanauer, with special thanks, pages 5, 13, 31, 32, 35
©Alistair Morrison/Sygma Photo News, pages 24, 51
©Nigel Parry/Creative Photographers, page 15
©Jeffery Thurnher/Outline Press Syndicate, pages 19, 21
Globe Photos: Fitzroy Barret; Dave Bennet, Alpha/Globe; Dave Chancellor, Alpha/Globe; Rose Hartman; Richard Open; Richard Slade

Theatrical photography ©Donald Cooper/Photostage England.

Personal photos courtesy of Carinthia West and Theadora van Runkle.

Film stills courtesy of the Academy of Motion Picture Arts and Sciences, Columbia Pictures, Globe Photos, Photofest, Warner Bros. Inc.
Age of Consent, courtesy of Columbia Pictures
Cal ©1984 Eastern Counties Newspapers Group Limited
Excalibur ©1981 Orion Pictures Company
The Mosquito Coast ©1986 The Saul Zaentz Company

Front and back cover photos courtesy of Granada Television.

We would also like to acknowledge Gwendolyn Pettus, Renate Stendhal, Zelda Zamanksi, Ray Souza, and a much-missed friend, the late David Stewart, for .support and inspiration.

SUPPORT YOUR LOCAL PUBLIC BROADCASTING STATION!

EVERY COMMUNITY ACROSS America is reached by one of the 346 member stations of the Public Broadcasting Service. These stations bring information, entertainment, and insight for the whole family.

THINK ABOUT THE programs you enjoy and remember most: *Mystery . . . Masterpiece Theatre . . . Nova . . . Nature . . . Sesame Street . . . Ghostwriter . . . Reading Rainbow . . . Baseball . . . The Civil War . . . MacNeil/Lehrer News Hour . . . Great Performances . . . Eyes on the Prize . . . National Geographic . . . Washington Week in Review . . .* and so many more.

ON YOUR LOCAL PBS station, you'll also find fascinating adult education courses, provocative documentaries, great cooking and do-it-yourself programs, and thoughtful local analysis.

DESPITE THE GENEROUS underwriting contributions of foundations and corporations, more than half of all public television budgets come from individual member support.

FOR LESS THAN THE cost of a night at the movies, less than a couple of months of a daily paper, less than a month of your cable TV bill, you can help make possible all the quality programming you enjoy.

BECOME A MEMBER of your public broadcasting station and do your part.

 Public Television. You make it happen!